The nature of
landscape design

The nature of landscape design

As an Art Form,
A Craft,
A Social Necessity

by Nan Fairbrother
with a Foreword by F. Fraser Darling

 Alfred A. Knopf   New York   1974

Grateful acknowledgment is given for permission to use the
following:

New England Village, Unknown American, from the Edgar William
and Bernice Chrysler Garbisch collection at the National Gallery of
Art, Washington, D.C. Reproduced by permission.

A Woodland Landscape, Jacob Van Ruisdael, at The Barber Institute
of Fine Arts, University of Birmingham, England. Reproduced by
permission.

Albrecht Dürer's study of hands and madness. Reproduced by
permission of the Robert Lehman Foundation, New York, New
York.

Library of Congress Cataloging in Publication Data

Fairbrother, Nan.   The nature of landscape design.

    1. Landscape architecture.   I. Title.
SB472.F3 1974   712   73-20758
ISBN 0-394-47046-X

MANUFACTURED IN THE UNITED STATES OF AMERICA
FIRST AMERICAN EDITION

To
Thelma Bates
and
Michael Cameron, my doctors,
without whose help this book
would not have been written

Contents

Foreword

Madame de Sévigné appears to me to be a symbol of feminine emancipation, possibly because she was articulate and inherently intellectual in an emerging society where the world of the mind was not looked upon as a purely masculine preserve. I also find that for me one of the charms of the seventeenth and eighteenth centuries is the salon, where women could show the versatility of their culture, where the very furniture was designed for conversation between the sexes. These women were of necessity amateurs, unknowing or contemptuous of the paper qualifications which rule us now and probably more widely read than some university graduates are today.

Nan Fairbrother, in our century, was of this company. Exquisite in person, generous in spirit and immediately apprehending in conversation, she was able to respond with a brilliance of clarity that brought any discussion into logical and illuminating perspective. I once saw her embarrassed by being described as a qualified landscape architect. She was too modest, but thank goodness her beautiful free mind had not been constricted by formal training. The discipline of her mind came from within, and those of us not altogether too vain or thick in the skull recognized that we were learning a discipline of landscape architecture from her.

This book was written during Nan Fairbrother's terminal illness, when she knew it would be a race against time. The fact of its being written at all is one of immense significance, something we cannot approach without wonder. What strength and courage sustained her? A primarily subjective approach in taking up this posthumous work is inevitable, but once we read so much as a page we realize that Nan Fairbrother's mind was at its best until the end, a triumphal progress through pain and adversity.

In life her conversation was eloquent and never empty, yet not so serious as to become pontifical or expounding in the truth she was compelled to tell. Her writing is like this also, deceptively conversational, splashed with wit and the apt phrase. She could not stand humbug or pretentiousness, so her book reads with the ease that makes it a natural testament of beauty. Of course, she would reprove me for saying "testament," but that is what it is.

She has called the book *The Nature of Landscape Design.* The "nature" of her title is the only word she could have used, for here are the anatomy and physiology of organic complexes and physical forms which we call landscape and which are the basis of such unconscious or intentional effects that we bring about through time and land use. You will not find a sentence as clumsy as this last one of mine throughout the book, but I have risked prolixity to explain accurately the depth of her understanding of the changes plants and animals create in landscape.

Nan Fairbrother was among the first to see the essential link between ecology and landscape design. I repeat, design. Sir Arthur Tansley's perceptive mind had made clear to us throughout his life—and especially in his monumental *The British Islands and Their Vegetation* (1939)—how deeply landscape was influenced by vegetation. Patrick Geddes in his day probed the whole subject of landscape and its organic structure. So had Frederick Law Olmsted, in America, and Vaughan Cornish, in his *Scenery and the Sense of Sight* (1935), brought out the link between tree form, land form and even roof form.

Had it fallen to Nan to become president of the British Ecological Society, I think the conjectural presidential address would have been one of those fruitful borderline discourses that are illuminating events in science. The ecologist recognizes that boundaries between habitats, "ecotones" in his jargon, are biologically rich and dynamic, gathering variety from both sides. It is the same with knowledge, a fact which should admonish our tendency to overspecialize.

Nan Fairbrother grasped the significance of the time factor to landscape, with its geological erosion, its soil making, and the ameliorating influence of the ultimate climax of vegetation over the initial geological limitations of what we might call "poor situations." Landscape *design* demands an intimate knowledge of natural history and the time factor (if only to save time) to save the results from being ludicrous. Landscape architecture is not just spatial, with organic masses trimmed to forms they cannot keep, as the eighteenth-century French were in some danger of interpreting it. It is an unfolding, carrying belief in the changes that the landscape desires to bring about—something akin to and producing the same results as traditional farming methods in several parts of England and Europe, which have unconsciously formed beautiful examples that carry the pleasing illusion of intentional design.

Although their lives overlapped for a few years in an intellectually exciting time, it is unlikely that Sir George Sitwell and Nan Fairbrother met each other; yet one of the imaginary conversations I should like to read would be between these two. Both were aesthetically sensitive and developed: Sir George's interest in the horizontals and planes could produce magnificent frameworks or skeletons for the landscape gardener, as you may read in his *On the Making of Gardens,* but I believe his conception of landscapes beyond the patrician garden was limited and almost puritanical. Even his own gardener thought Sir George's idea of a garden was "anaemic." Perhaps the owner of coal-getting country in the past could not see landscape in Nan Fairbrother's sense at all, but merely as something which shielded him, yet gave him the illusion of space. Sir George, looking over the great industrial valley of Sheffield to Lord Fitzwilliam's seat occasionally visible over the smoke, could say, "There is nothing between Renishaw and Wentworth." The murky valley, with its hundreds of thousands of human beings, chimneys and whatnot, was as nothing. Nan's conception of landscapes started from nature, from a ready acceptance that in a country inhabited by human beings, landscape would inevitably be modified. To this was added the profound truth that landscape influences all aspects of human life and psyche. Therefore, landscape was a living thing to be understood as a physician knows his patients and their communal life. Her landscape architecture has become an essential part of human ecology, the aspect of that science which academics have but recently admitted.

Conservation as ecology in action is emerging into an attitude of mind that is far ahead of its slightly encapsulated, nature-loving origins. There was something a trifle precious and selfish in the old view of what passed as conservation. In fact, there has been evidence in the last year or two of a mistaken proletarian backlash, from the darkness of the cities, that conservation stands for elitism and privilege. I can think of no clearer statement than this book of the fallacy of such a warped view, yet its author remained always sympathetic to those who wonder in their state of unknowing whether the growing ethic of care for nature may deprive them still more. *The Nature of Landscape Design* is also something of an essay in good housekeeping, how man and nature must co-exist if either is to survive, how our furniture can be arranged and rearranged for greater convenience, economy of space and resources, and enlightening enjoyment. It also shows another of Nan Fairbrother's gifts, the ability to choose her illustrations with an aptness and precision that make them an integral part of the work, rather than incidental decorative interpolations.

Nan Fairbrother's amalgam of art and science in an organic setting is something that proliferating mankind intensely needs if the species is to be human humanely. A great deal of what she had to say was in her *New Lives, New Landscapes,* but this book reflects her deeper intellectual search into the physiology of land-scape and the psychology of human beings in relation to it. In a world where we are seeing increasingly clearly the dangers of too many human beings, she recognized the significance of space and enclosure, caring passionately for the well-being of people who are to endure or enjoy landscape.

Frank Fraser Darling

November, 1973
Lauchyhill, Forres, Moray, Scotland

The nature of
landscape design

1.
Introduction

Man is an animal who consciously creates landscape: the only species which deliberately alters the design of its environment for no other reason than to give itself aesthetic pleasure. Other creatures reshape their surroundings—grazing animals change forest to grassland, beavers build dams which create lakes and swamps—but this is incidental in the ordinary way of survival; only man deliberately rearranges the setting he lives in simply because he prefers the look of it.

As human beings we have many specific qualities which separate us from the rest of the animal world, and this nonfunctional concern with our surroundings is one of the most distinctive. We respond profoundly to our environment, and this quite apart from its potential for food or shelter or any other of our practical animal needs. A large part of our pleasure in holidays, for instance, is simply in the change of setting, and though we take this for granted it is by no means an obvious pleasure. After all, there are more straightforward delights—we might eat more or drink more or sleep more or make love more—but if that were all, then holidays at home would do us, and we could save ourselves all the effort and expense of crowded travel to crowded places which are seldom as comfortable as the homes we left.

But in fact the essence of going on a holiday is being somewhere else experiencing a different environment. And most of what we do on holiday is exactly that—we walk about, or sit about, or travel about, and simply enjoy the savour of different surroundings.

Nor is this nonpractical concern with our environment mere holiday escapism. As every estate agent knows, a poor house in good surroundings will sell for a higher price than a better house in poor surroundings, and in a town they confidently ask 25 percent more rent for a flat with a view of a park than for an identical flat with no view. We value our surroundings for aesthetic reasons—amenity reasons—whatever we like to call them.

THE NATURE OF LANDSCAPE DESIGN

Landscape design is concerned with the process of creating attractive outdoor environments; but it is easier to state this as a fact than to describe specifically what it means. For to begin with, what do we mean by landscape? A landscape is not simply an area of the earth's surface, a square on a map irrespective of human existence. The *Oxford English Dictionary* defines it as "a prospect of inland scenery, such as can be taken in at a glance from one point of view," and this at once brings in the essential human element— "prospect," "glance," "point of view"—the idea of a composition. For a landscape is not an area but our vision of that area; we ourselves, as the seeing eye, are included in the concept, and our reactions are an essential part of the combination. In the various current systems of landscape evaluation many in fact evaluate not the landscape itself, but our human response to it—is it of high or low scenic value? Beautiful or ugly? Do we in fact like the look of it? As a way of assessing which areas are most worth protecting this may be excellent, but it tells us more about ourselves as viewers than about the view. The mountain scenery, for instance, which many people now admire above all other, was once detested as dreary wastes. Certainly as an analysis of the scene itself assessment by our own reactions tells us little: nothing of the landscape's origin or purpose or composition, or of the basic material with which landscape design is concerned, although these are the underlying essentials for any useful understanding of landscape.

If we define the creation of landscape as man's manipulation of the outdoor scene to produce a different kind of landscape to suit his own uses, then this is a definition which covers all our activities, from managing natural forests for timber, clearing trees to grow crops, building urban and industrial areas, to laying out gardens round our houses. These either derive directly from the natural scene and its resources or depend upon man's management of it, and to evaluate any landscape we therefore need to understand both its present function and its origin in terms of man's activity.

CATEGORIES OF LANDSCAPE TYPE

Most areas can be analysed in terms of three fundamental categories. First are the landscapes derived more or less directly from the natural habitat of the region—forest, desert, and so on.

In their pure form these exist only where man is absent, but where the human population is scarce and does not live by working the land, then the habitat may be little changed from its natural state. This is clearly so where, for instance, primitive people live by hunting, but also to a lesser extent where an advanced industrial population lives in settlements divorced from the areas which support it, as now increasingly is the case in the deserts of western America.

The second category of landscape is that produced by man's alteration of the natural habitat for his own uses, generally without concern for the scenery as such. The obvious example here is farming, which all over the world has replaced the original landscape with a very different scenery of fields and crops. On a smaller scale, and more recently, industry and urban areas are producing landscapes even more radically changed from the natural habitat.

In the third category is landscape which has been deliberately designed, until now generally for pleasure. Parks and gardens belong here, as well as various new types of what we now call amenity landscape.

Very few areas, however, belong to one single category. Woodland, although it may seem natural, has generally been influenced by man, as in eastern America, where most woodland is regrowth after felling of the original forests. Equally the farming countryside, though a man-made landscape created from forest by land use, is still governed by what crops will grow in the habitat, and will generally include areas of more or less natural vegetation. Most areas, in fact, are a combination of all three types interacting to produce landscapes for the benefit of the human beings who live in them. In the past the third category—the consciously designed —has been unimportant in the general scene, and also of very minor extent; but increasingly now this conscious concern is spreading to landscape in general, and it is our only hope for the future, that we should realise what we are doing to the whole of our surroundings and take deliberate action to make them pleasant to live in.

THE NEW DIMENSION

Historically, landscape design has been one of the fine arts, finding expression in formal Renaissance gardens and the private parks of the eighteenth century. That landscape should have any

Man-made landscape—farm land in Dorset.

Man-designed landscape—city park (Regent's Park, London).

A three-category landscape: more or less natural habitat in the beech woods; agricultural land use in the fields; deliberate design in the eighteenth-century layout and twentieth-century conservation (London's Green Belt, between Amersham and Beaconsfield).

function other than an aesthetic or an agricultural one—that it should be designed for what we now call amenity—would have seemed strange to past societies, for, insofar as it was not laid out to give pleasure to a select few, it was the concern of working farmers (or in more sparsely populated areas, where the natural habitat was more or less planned by man, it was presumably the concern of God). Certainly farmers planned their landscapes consciously and carefully—clearing trees, enclosing fields, arranging the pattern of pasture and arable, of enclosures, of woodlots for farm timber, of access roads for working the land, and so on. But this was the practical organisation of a working area, and if appearance was considered it was incidental. Nonetheless the old methods of farming produced beautiful and harmonious landscapes—created, for instance, the English countryside we still cherish and the old New England landscape Americans still look back to with affection.

This happy and spontaneous combination of use and beauty was the amenity landscape of its day, but the circumstances which produced it have been disrupted by the changed conditions of our new society. Farming is now a minor land use in eastern America, while in Britain the old farming countryside is changing with new farming methods. More urban than any generation before and moving to an even more urbanised future, most of us now live in man-made environments, which many people feel to be unnatural conditions. Our lives now are very much further from nature than was eighteenth-century society, and although no one now would tolerate the living conditions of the old rural life, many people consciously regret the loss of contact with anything like a natural habitat. Certainly one universal use of leisure in modern industrial societies is escape to surroundings nearer to nature. Like persons in the eighteenth century we too sigh for the Simple Life, even though our motorcar, caravan, convenience-food version is no more simple than their equally urban but more elegant fancies, such as Marie Antoinette's dairy.

But whatever the urban accessories, our longing for the country is real: it is a genuine desire for the natural rather than the man-made, and from this fundamental reaction to our new

Our towns leafier.

Our suburbs more countrified.

Our country more natural. All three by deliberate design.

urban habitat could come a genuine new style of landscape design—the Natural. We can no longer, as those in the eighteenth century (who would certainly have spelt it with a capital N), create fine-art landscapes to express a new conception of ideal scenery, but for our applied-art landscapes we could work out methods to disguise our growing domination of our environment, to use natural arrangements of landscape material, and to live with plants on their own free-growing terms. This is what we are now trying to work out, for though we still want—and more than ever before—the natural habitat enhanced, the relief we need in the modern world is not from the natural but from the urban habitat. We want our cities more leafy, our suburbs more countrified, our countryside wilder—all our landscapes, in fact, transposed from the man-made towards the natural. The Natural.

So much for the aspirations; how to achieve them? One principle is clear. Landscape is essentially the physical expression of land use, and it is with land use that we must begin. This does not mean turning one's back on industrialisation or on the needs of the society it has produced. Rather, it involves working with a

All land forms (Blea Tann, Lake District).

range of methods that reflect the many and varied uses to which land is now put. Most modern landscapes are working landscapes, and even amenity areas must generally include things like sports fields, playgrounds, cafés, shelters, and assortments of buildings. The role of the designer is to evolve, out of all the conflicting claims of use and amenity, a landscape that will still be pleasant for the user. An earlier book, *New Lives, New Landscapes,* was an attempt to see how this could be done and to suggest what controls might be appropriate to this end. The present book is specifically about this new conception of landscape and its design and management, and particularly about the latter factors. For while use is the starting point, nevertheless the actual physical arrangement of the landscape material—land forms, water, vegetation, and man-made structures—should be undertaken as a creative exercise evolving in the first place from a consideration of the interacting complex of climate, geology, wildlife, and all the other elements in the natural scene, including (and especially important for landscape design) the vegetation natural to the region.

In all our surroundings this last factor is fundamental. In

All vegetation (Chilthern beech woods).

All man-made structures (New York).

But most landscape is a combination of all three (Amersham churchyard).

organic landscapes it is clearly essential to know what nature would produce without us, but even in the built landscape it governs what effects we want, what plants will grow, whether maintenance will consist of encouraging or restraining their growth, and so on. The habitat, in fact, is the basic foundation of every design, whether it closely resembles the natural scenery or whether we create entirely different surroundings.

The greater the transformation, however, the less we are concerned with the original landscape—comparatively little, for instance, in cities, more in gardens, more still in parks and country areas, and very closely concerned in design for wild landscapes like the national parks. Even the "wild" areas themselves may need managing to keep them wild, as is already accepted in the American national parks and increasingly now in Britain, and this can be done only by first understanding the natural habitat.

Such management will become increasingly important in the future, especially since our increasing areas of amenity landscape seem likely to please us best if their design is as close as possible to the natural landscape. At present, however, there is little information about naturalistic design as compared with the design of gardens and park-style landscapes, and the next chapter is therefore a discussion of the natural habitat in relation to landscape design.

2.
The basic material

The natural habitats of the world—the deserts and grasslands and forests—are distributed round the globe in very roughly parallel bands. These are affected by diverse local conditions, such as height, or large land masses, or the nearness of oceans, but nonetheless they are primarily determined by latitude. It is the distance from the equator which produces the variations in temperature and hours of daylight which, interacting with the geology, will to a great extent determine the land forms, vegetation, and wildlife of an area.

LANDSCAPE ZONES

Since vegetation, or its lack, is for many purposes a useful yardstick, the different zones can be broadly classified by their vegetation types into tropical forest (nearest the equator), savanna, desert, steppe, evergreen trees and shrubs, temperate deciduous forest, conifer forest, and tundra (nearest the poles). It is obvious that human beings do not equally occupy all these habitats. We are not naturally adapted to extremes of heat or cold, and extreme habitats do not produce the necessary food supply. Man as a species seems to have evolved in the tropics, and when human societies eventually developed they were chiefly in warm regions. The early civilisations based on farming were mostly at or near Mediterranean latitudes—the cultures of northern India, the civilisations of the Tigris-Euphrates basin and of the eastern Mediterranean. It was from its origin in these latitudes that farming later spread north into the cooler habitats of the temperate woodlands. The first farmers chiefly lived in the regions lying north of the deserts, in the semi-arid zone of evergreen trees and shrubs, which has now mostly disappeared, destroyed by the centuries of grazing and ploughing of successive agricultural civilisations.

But if a warm climate best suited the crops of agricultural man, it seems not to have best suited the type of man who produced the next great change in human society. For industrial man did not develop in Mediterranean latitudes: the Industrial Revolution began on a cool rainy island off the coast of temperate Europe, and its early spread and explosive growth was equally in the countries of the temperate zone. Even now, with all the world moving towards an industrialised state, the advanced societies are still chiefly in the zones of temperate forest. And it is in these regions that the impact of man on the natural habitat can most clearly be seen.

MAN'S IMPACT ON THE NATURAL HABITAT

Human beings have been altering their habitats ever since they left the primitive hunter stage. Farmers and their changing land uses have produced a long succession of different landscapes, each developing from the other—pastoral landscapes became arable landscapes, regressed or developed with variations of climate and the changing fortunes of agriculture and state of society. In Britain the small fields of the Celtic farmers became the large open fields of the Anglo-Saxons; with enclosure these were divided up by hedges and rows of trees which are now disappearing again, and the agricultural landscape is returning to a more open appearance. In other countries the changes have been different, but except in areas only recently occupied by modern man, such as the American West, the present scene is generally far removed from anything which existed before man appeared. Moreover, as well as the deliberate actions of man which change the landscape, there are also the changes which result from his very existence, his need to move from place to place, his need for shelter, and his increasing numbers.

Nonetheless the changes caused by man are seldom permanent changes, though there are sometimes situations where the reestablishing vegetation will differ in various ways from the original, as can be seen in the second-growth woodland of northeastern America, which differs from the original forest. Likewise there are situations where, as in the drained fens of East Anglia, a fundamental change in the soil structure has been made. But there is always, in the existing conditions of an area, an inherent type of vegetation which would reestablish without our help, and which in this discussion is considered as the natural. A knowledge and understanding of this natural potential of any area is essential for the design and management of landscape, which should not be an exercise in abstract principles but the creation of a particular kind of outdoor environment from the materials available and in the conditions prevailing.

LOWLAND BRITAIN AND NORTHEASTERN AMERICA

In areas of human settlement the natural vegetation has been modified by the shifting patterns of man's use, and it is only where man has moved away for good that it returns and reverts to its original form. This process can best be illustrated by comparing lowland Britain and the northeastern United States, which despite considerable differences in climate are alike in their vegetation—deciduous woodland—and share a common European cultural heritage, with similar attitudes to landscape.

The natural woodlands of lowland Britain are various, but chiefly oak and its associates, and though originally the tree line reached as high as 2,000 feet the present one is nearer 1,500. Since, however, we chiefly live in the lowlands, the difference is irrelevant, and most man-designed landscapes replace a natural habitat of deciduous woodland. So they do equally in eastern America, though here the types of woodland are more various and the species of trees far more numerous. They include broad-leaved evergreens as well as conifers, both on high ground and on poor soils, and also the early stages of regrowth of deciduous woodland.

In Britain it is certainly not obvious that in a state of nature our countryside would be covered with trees, and many believe that our natural landscape is grassland. But this only proves how thoroughly man the farmer has altered the original habitat, and that the countryside we inherited from past generations is as man-made as the towns.

In northeastern America, however, no one could doubt that forest is the natural landscape, for woodland is everywhere and covers more than half the land area. We realise this even when travelling on roads with their accompanying development, and from the air the land seems a vast expanse of woodland interspersed and infiltrated by built-up urban areas, with here and there openings which are water or farms. And the woodland is clearly spontaneous: it is what happens when no one interferes; and since it is also what would potentially happen in Britain, awareness of this should always be present in our landscape designs. But it is difficult to visualise this potential forest in a countryside where only 8

Hundreds of acres of cereals, but nonetheless trees are the natural vegetation (Oxfordshire).

percent of the land surface is wooded (compared with 29 percent for the rest of Europe) and where even the hedgerow trees are disappearing as modern mechanised farming bulldozes the old hedges.

These wide differences in the existing landscapes of the two countries are due to different land use and planning policies, and are comparatively recent developments. The original countryside which the early settlers created in America was similar to England's; it was a farming landscape of fields and woods—more woods admittedly in newly occupied America than in long-denuded England, but essentially similar farmland scenery, and the name New England described the countryside as well as the society. This is the life and landscape which America looks back to with nostalgia, and it is easy to see why from the delightful paintings of little towns with their strong sense of identity, set among the fields and woods which supported them. The early settlers had no choice but to grow the food they needed, but much of the area is not good farmland—certainly not the rocky soil of New England—and

farming was never an easy or profitable living. During the nineteenth century the frontier was pushed westwards into the vast and
fertile cornlands of the prairies, and as transportation improved,
grain was sent eastwards. The small eastern farms, whose rocky soil
posed physical obstacles to the use of machinery, could not compete
with the huge mechanised farms in the Midwest. Much of the
eastern farmland was therefore abandoned and the trees came back,
spreading from the woodlots and thickets into the empty pastures
and deserted ploughland, and enveloping the old farming countryside with a high green fleece of woods. In New England stone walls

Nineteenth-century New England. (New England Village, *Unknown American.*)

running half-hidden through the trees are still witness of the vanished farming countryside—ghostly reminders like the village fire
alarms which sound so eerily like the lowing of vanished cows—and
old people there can still remember a landscape of open fields in
areas now tall with trees.

Locally small areas of agricultural land are still worked for
highly perishable or specialised crops, and in some areas in Pennsylvania farming is still a way of life that provides self-sufficiency,
but elsewhere the reversion to forest in these abandoned areas goes
on. Despite the inroads of urban development, the potential of the

One of the remaining farms in Connecticut.

Most of the field walls are now lost in woodland.

regenerating of forest areas for recreation, both for active sports like shooting and for driving about the countryside for pleasure, has greatly increased.

In Britain the situation is different, for our arable farms are better suited to modernisation than many of those in north-eastern America and our climate allows our livestock farmers to grow the best grass in the world. These facts, combined with a marked change in agricultural policy towards greater self-suffi-ciency, make farming still a very positive factor in the countryside. If eastern United States had to produce as much food per acre as we do in Britain, then the scenery in the Northeast would be very different and still probably much like ours. Certainly in Britain it is easy to believe that trees are something added to a natural ground cover of grass, but the fact remains that grass and other crops are really growing in forest clearings. The forest may not be there at present—there may not in fact be a single tree in the landscape—but that is incidental. If we left the area alone, whether in a city centre or a bare hilltop, it would ultimately change to woodland.

THE TEMPERATE FOREST HABITAT AND ITS DEVELOPMENT

Though it is the presence of man which most fundamentally affects things, vegetation itself of course is in a state of constant change. In a forest climate trees are clearly the dominant form of plant life, the highest development of the habitat. But they are not the only vegetation, for a great many other plants grow in associa-tion with them, either at intermediate stages of woodland develop-ment or adapted to the woodland habitat.

Furthermore, though woodland may be the natural state of most temperate landscapes, it is only the ultimate state, for between bare ground and the eventual establishment of woodland there are various progressions. Very briefly, bare ground changes to woodland by the taller plants suppressing the lower—by the successive growth of herbs (which include grasses), then shrubs, then trees, each higher stage of the vegetation crowding out, or at least controlling, the lower forms.

As every gardener knows, uncut short grass soon becomes long grass with its associated flowers, and as every farmer knows, unmown long grass soon becomes scrub, which will be gradually invaded by trees and grow up to woodland. For all vegetation strives towards a balanced "climax" which is relatively stable, and in our climate this is forest. In the natural landscape herbs and shrubs seldom occur alone as permanent vegetation as they do in our man-made landscapes, but are either plants in woodland or stages in the regrowth of woodland destroyed by tree fall, fire, flood, landslide, or other natural hazards. These intermediate vegetation types therefore are unstable and can be maintained only by man's interference.

Natural temperate woodlands vary with soil and situation, and each type consists of specific groups of flowers, grasses, shrubs, and trees. And not only does each kind of woodland have a characteristic group of plants, but there are also different kinds of vegetation in its various stages of development. The flowers and shrubs which precede one type of woodland are different from those which precede another: more than that, the plants change as the progress to woodland develops; newcomers are not simply added to the plants already established, but the flowers, for instance, of one stage of development are different from those of preceding or succeeding stages.

For plants grow in communities of different species which either enjoy similar conditions or create conditions suitable for one another's needs. A group of plants which needs full sunlight does not survive the growth of trees, whereas woodland plants need tree shelter and the humus of fallen leaves. In the same way birch is a common pioneer tree in open ground in Britain, as pines are in eastern America, though both tend to disappear as the woodland develops and shade becomes denser. When we plant trees we alter the conditions and therefore the vegetation, and we can see this in our man-made landscapes, where the shade of growing trees suppresses meadow grasses and other light-loving plants, and encourages other species which survive the shade. Planting trees is thus one way of managing the lower layers of vegetation, since the growth of the woodland floor is far less vigorous and is easier to control than the vegetation of open ground in full sun.

TEMPERATE WOODLAND AS LANDSCAPE

If we wish to create a different landscape from nature's own, it requires effort on our part not only to create the landscape but also to maintain it in that condition; otherwise it would gradually revert back to its "natural" state. Thus the less the effort available, the nearer our design must be to the landscape natural to the area. Or if the statement is more convincing in reverse, then the nearer the landscape is to natural, the easier it is to create and look after, since nature is working on our side. In Britain and northeast America, this usually means woodland, and trees are not only easy to grow, but woodland as the final stage of the vegetation's development is the only landscape which is relatively stable. Other types of scenery would be at some intermediate stage—whether natural or man-made—in a progressive change: they are in a state of arrested development. There is, of course, inherent instability in any community of living plants, for in a woodland, trees will fall as they grow old. Light will penetrate the forest floor, and secondary succession will begin as the gap ultimately is filled again by one of the dominant woodland tree species.

In northeastern America the various stages of plant succession—from open fields to forest—are to be seen, and many areas have already reached the second-growth version of the indigenous forest, which is the natural landscape in present conditions. In Britain, too, sceptics who still feel that grass is natural could easily be convinced by removing the controls—farming, grazing, heather-burning, and so on—and watching what happens. The specific landscape—farmland, downland, moorland—would disappear swiftly or gradually depending on local conditions, and the change begin which would eventually bring about the return to woodland. This can be seen well in downland areas traditionally grazed by sheep, in many of which barley is now grown. The steeper slopes, where machinery cannot go, and which are no longer grazed, are gradually becoming covered in scrub. Woodland, if left alone, would still be woodland centuries hence (as by then would also be most of our other landscapes, even our cities). But this does not mean that woodland as landscape for man's use needs no maintenance whatsoever. Depending on its use it needs undergrowth cleared, dead wood removed, regeneration assisted, and so forth. Nonetheless, since this is the climax vegetation, maintenance is far less and far simpler than for other types of landscape.

Apart from its own considerable merits woodland is also an excellent basis for other types of landscape and can be quickly adapted, producing a visually mature landscape in far less time than any other process. For removing trees is, alas, a very much simpler operation than growing them, and a design based on

New England succession—grazed fields, rough grass, scrub, conifer, and mixed woodland (Connecticut).

making clearings in woodland is much sooner achieved than one based on planting trees in open areas.

Woodland is easily changed to a varied design of masses and spaces simply by clearing areas of trees, encouraging those left to thicken into clumps, and establishing rough grass on the open spaces. This creates a bold seminatural landscape which stands considerable wear, and which is a useful setting for many kinds of development and land use—as, for example, recreation in London's Epping Forest.

Woodland serves equally well as a framework for other landscapes. It is easily adapted to subtle garden effects and sheltered privacy by making openings among the trees and laying out paths and flowers and chosen shrubs. The maintenance of such woodland gardens is low, since the setting of trees needs little attention, and labour is concentrated on creating special effects within the natural framework of the area and maintaining an intermediate stage of succession in the woodland clearings.

Woodland managed for recreation. Paths and open space in the New Forest, Hampshire.

A garden made from existing woodland by clearing vegetation and opening vistas through the trees. Early-morning frost on the grass (Lyme, Conn.).

THE STABILITY OF LANDSCAPE—MANAGEMENT AND MAINTENANCE

In most landscapes, certainly in a temperate climate, design is concerned not with climax forest but with the preforest stages, which are essentially unstable. Thus, if layout is a matter of arranging the masses and spaces of the vegetation, then maintenance consists of controlling the natural changes in this arrangement.

For a landscape is not a once-only creation in inert materials, but a living composition in constant process of change to a different state—if not of growing, then of dying. It has its own inherent patterns of survival which nature constantly reinstates, and for any different design to survive, control is needed to check or reverse them.

Even in woodland there are some changes, certainly if our trees are not those of the natural forest of the area; but unless our different choice is wildly unsuitable they are likely to be slow. In landscapes based on earlier stages of the succession—grass and flowers and shrubs—the changes will be far more active, and will be not only towards the substitution of local plants for ours, but also towards the next stage in the growth of our own vegetation. Our design in fact will become more "natural" (or more "weedy" and "overgrown"—it depends on the point of view). In either case it is necessary to realise what spontaneous changes are likely, both for planning a system of maintenance to suit the design and for using efficient methods to keep the cost to a minimum.

In considering plants as landscape material we commonly think in terms of the different layers of the vegetation—flowers and shrubs and trees—as completely different entities. They are in fact far more separate in our minds (and in our plant catalogues) than they commonly are in nature; and in our man-made landscapes, if there is to be a definite distinction between trees and hedges, between hedges and flowers, between flowers and grass, this will in itself form a considerable part of maintenance (mowing grass, for instance, to prevent its growing up to an herb layer). Unless this is done, the design becomes blurred and eventually lost.

In small-scale gardens this is clearly so. If the vegetation were left to grow for a year—no grass mown, no beds weeded, no shrubs cut back—then the garden would scarcely exist in garden terms as generally understood; even a holiday absence in a rainy summer can produce a well-established revolution.

In larger landscapes the changes take longer, but the design equally depends on definition of the layers; the farming countryside, for instance, is created by the clear definition of herb-layer fields, shrub-layer hedges, and tree-layer woods. The defining of the "layers" is used here as a way of controlling the succession of the vegetation, and is in fact the commonest method of control in man-made landscape. Other methods—clear felling of trees, burning of scrub—do not maintain the landscape in its existing state but put the area back to square one, where the succession starts all over again.

In most landscapes, however, this is clearly undesirable. What we generally need is not a series of stages in the succession to woodland, but a permanent mosaic of the different stages, and this we commonly hold static by defining the layers and preventing their further growth (mowing grass, cutting hedges, and so on).

As a general rule the higher the layer the more resistant it is to change and to invasion by plants of the succeeding stage, and also the slower the growth of the invaders (weeds take over flowerbeds, for instance, much faster than shrubs invade grass, or trees turn scrub to woodland). It is the early stages of the succession which are most quickly established and which are also the most difficult to manage. It is easier to keep long grass than short, easier to get rid of shrubs than herb-layer weeds, and easiest to get rid of trees. Like animals, the smaller and more ubiquitous the more difficult to control: we long ago dealt with the wolves, but the rats are still very much with us.

Flowerbeds need more labour than any other part of the landscape because we grow flowers in open soil to free them from competition. And if it is unnatural to prevent vegetation from developing to a higher layer, then to prevent vegetation from growing at all is, in a fertile climate, to defy nature's basic economy.

In desert conditions plants may grow dotted out with bare ground between them, but not in temperate zones. Here vegetation covers the whole of the land surface, and bare soil scarcely ever occurs in natural conditions. Bare soil is, in fact, a pressing invitation to vegetation to move in, which it rapidly does. And since the plants we choose to grow are often vulnerable introductions, we protect them from the natives (i.e., weeds) by keeping the earth bare round them. But clearly our aim should not be to keep the ground bare but to fill it with plants of our own choosing, for in a fertile climate open soil is like an inviting house standing empty in a crowded city—if someone doesn't move in legally then someone will move in illegally. Weeds are squatters, and if we don't want them we should not leave any place for them to squat.

The use of ground-cover plants eliminates bare earth without introducing serious competition and is commonly recommended as a simple solution. But since the ground-cover plants must be less vigorous than the native vegetation, they will in their turn need weeding. There is no way of substituting our own design for nature's except by providing effort. The best we can do is reduce the effort to a minimum by applying it where it produces the greatest effect within the natural processes of change.

THE STABILITY OF LANDSCAPE—DIVERSITY AND WILDLIFE

A "natural" landscape is diverse; it contains a very large number of both plant and animal species. Man's interference in the natural landscape results in the loss of a large number of these species, leading to a much simpler, less diverse community. In the agricultural landscape the final stage of this process is a weed-free cropland, where a single crop is being grown extensively.

This in itself creates an unstable situation, for diseases or insect pests in such a situation can reach epidemic proportions rapidly without the natural checks which would occur in a more diverse landscape. Predators are often absent because a host species vital in their life cycle is not present. Lack of diversity of plant species in a habitat will also result in lack of diversity of wildlife, and many conservationists are very seriously concerned that some of our landscapes are becoming so "simple" as to pose a threat to wildlife. The change from traditional mixed farming, where a large number of crops were grown in small fields (hedges giving considerable diversity of habitat), to a simpler, more intensive form of farming, with fewer crops and larger fields, is a cause for great concern.

The planting of native vegetation, of plant associations within their correct habitats, would make a very large contribution to the biological health of the landscape. Our native trees and shrubs support much larger and more diverse an insect population than do exotic species, and it would be well to remember that man's ability to adapt himself to different environments is not shared by other wildlife! The planting of native species in recognised plant associations would create valuable wildlife habitats to compensate for many being lost by the new farming methods.

TROUBLE-FREE PLANTING

If an understanding of the natural development of an area is the basis of easy maintenance, then equally the basis of trouble-free planting is the vegetation indigenous to the area. In choosing plants for any landscape it is useful to know what would naturally grow in the conditions we create, but in landscaping of any extent, especially if maintenance is limited, it is not so much useful as essential to know what plants would appear spontaneously and look after themselves.

Far more often than we suppose, this natural vegetation could be adapted to suit our design, but certainly not always, for our plants must suit the landscape's purposes as well as the locality. Nonetheless the natural vegetation is what we are displacing, and the plants we choose must be vigorous enough to survive in competition.

Natural self-regenerating woodland, for instance, will clearly consist of trees specific to the particular area. In Britain, however, various other kinds of woodland have been planted through the centuries for various reasons, and when well suited to the conditions they have become established as seminatural.

Equally in other types of landscape we can either choose native plants different from the trees dominant in the natural habitat (for most woodland has many associated species) or else use plants introduced from areas with similar conditions.

This is what a nurseryman's catalogue does for gardeners in a rough-and-ready, hit-or-miss way by listing plants for particular situations—sun or shade, moist or dry, and so on. But many of these (apart from being plants the nurseryman has for sale rather than necessarily the most suitable choice) are in any case plants for gardens. They are to be sheltered, weeded, perhaps watered, certainly protected from all but the mildest competition. Only the most vigorous of garden plants or sometimes particular species exactly suited to particular conditions (those which establish themselves in the wild as garden escapees) survive for long in free competition with local vegetation. Plants in gardening catalogues are mostly either exotics (i.e., introduced from abroad) or else garden forms developed in nurseries; in either case their flowers are usually the chief concern, and since most of them are unsuitable for landscapes, where they must survive with minimum maintenance, we need other sources of information.

Ideally, of course, when deciding what to plant we should simply go and see what is growing naturally in the area of our landscape, but this is generally unrealistic. Even supposing there is vegetation—and some sites are virtually barren—it is unlikely (at least in Britain) to be natural to the area. It is quite possible, in fact, that nowhere in the neighbourhood is there a single plant which would be there in a state of nature.

So we can find our way as best we can only by starting from first essentials—by finding out all we can about the conditions of the site, particularly of soil texture and acidity, ground water, local climate, changes resulting from development, and so on. Given this information and armed with a knowledge of the land use proposed and the care available, we must make our selection.

Ecologists, too, can be of great help here, especially now that it is realised that ecology is no longer a matter of seeking out an area undisturbed by man and studying it in static isolation—that man is a vital part of the rapidly changing ecological systems all over the world, and that nothing is now static or isolated or free from human interference.

Ecologists, therefore, are invaluable in landscape design. Beginning with the original landscape natural to the area, they can tell us what differences are likely to develop in the changed conditions of man's occupation, they can deduce the stages the area is likely to go through in reaching this potentially ultimate state, and they can suggest how these natural processes could be most simply and satisfactorily controlled to produce the landscape we want. Ecologists in fact can provide most of the information which must underlie good design.

3.
Design
considerations

Thus far the effect of natural habitat on landscape design has been considered in practical terms of organising the actual material of landscape, but since our human reaction to what we see is also an essential part of the design, the effect of the habitat on the people who live in it is important as well. Our response to the man-made scene is conditioned by our experience of the natural scenery which surrounds us.

In an arid climate, for instance, where desert is the norm, lush vegetation is a vivid delight, a precious luxury in the sterile habitat, and the pleasure of the small irrigated gardens of the Middle East with their water and flowers and thriving green is more intense than it could ever be in a fertile climate where flowers and green abound. Our reactions to sun and shade, coolness and warmth, and so on equally depend on their context. Is a close grove of cedars a dank and gloomy tunnel in a forest landscape where leaves shut out the cheerful sun? Or is it a cool relief from an outside world where "the fierce heat dries up the moisture in the mouth, and the scorching wind consumes the very marrow of the bones"? Depending on where we live, or even the sort of day it is, our feelings about it might be quite different.

HUMAN REACTION TO LANDSCAPE—IMPLICATIONS FOR THE DESIGNER

Landscape design can be based on our reaction to the surrounding habitat in two different ways: either by enhancing the natural scenery or by providing relief from it. In an arid climate, such as southern California, this could consist of a large-scale desert-based design of sparse and carefully placed desert vegetation and rocks, in a ground surface of perhaps naked sand and gravel —and for the relief, the antithesis enhanced by its desert setting, a green canyon lush with the near-tropic vegetation which thrives in these fertile defiles, but made even lusher and more lavishly exuberant by water. This would be landscape in terms of the habitat, a freer version of the Middle East gardens, whose green charm is equally enhanced by the surrounding desert.

But if in this same context the landscape were an arbitrary composition of grass spaces and introduced vegetation maintained by watering, then it would lose all local feeling. It might be an excellently composed design, but it could be anywhere. There would be no specific experience of either desert or relief from desert; and no matter what its other merits, since it had no relation to the habitat, it would be a landscape of missed opportunities.

Certainly we must allow for the fact that an arid landscape lacks manageable mass and that introduced vegetation supported by watering may be inevitable. But if water is added—as it so often is in that kind of garden—by sprays and underground pipes, then it is not being used as it should be—for the pleasure of the water, as it is in Middle Eastern gardens.

Most landscape, in fact, in western America seems designed by people with a European landscape tradition developed in a temperate climate—a tradition of grass and flowers and trees and shrubs freely growing wherever they suit the design. It is the landscape of a fertile land, and the conception is not changed for the desert. In a forest climate, as opposed to desert, the enhancement and relief will be completely different. The enhancement will be of woodland glades, flowering paths, beautifully grouped trees, dappled sunlight. The relief, on the other hand, will be open space— the wide views and sense of freedom in open country, especially in hills, clearings in forests, the expanses of open lawn which are often the heart of the garden in temperate countries, and on yet a smaller scale the exactly kept hedges and low beds of flowers which please us by indicating the orderly control of vegetation naturally given to overgrowth.

The whole basis of landscape design changes with habitat. It will be different for grassland climates, for cold regions with conifers and long-lying snow, for tropical forest, and so on; and as landscape design spreads into new areas it will develop styles reflecting the region.

This is what Burle Marx is doing in Brazil and, far more than the merit of his designs, is why his work is important. In a tropical climate he enhances the habitat by lavish use of exuberantly growing plants chosen from the wide range of tropical vegetation (astonishingly wide compared with the limited temperate flora) and grown to perfection to display their great natural beauties. The relief he provides is from the overexuberance of tropical plants, from the sense of being overwhelmed by jungly growth. He does this by firmly controlled designs of abstract shapes, where plants are used as in-filling and are strictly disciplined to man's imposed pattern.

Indeed, the ideal of landscape design could be said to be that it makes us experience more vividly the natural scenery of the region we are in—that it intensifies our consciousness of the local habitat by defining its essential qualities, by both enhancing them and providing their antithesis. This is surely what eighteenth-century designers meant when they said that the true concern of landscape design was to express the *genius loci*. Habitat is a wider and vaguer concept than a single local place (twentieth-century air travel compared with an eighteenth-century coach), but the principle is the same—to convert to poetry the prose of the surrounding landscape.

At the design stage the choice of plants is unimportant, except that they serve as material for the composition. A collection of choice plants is not a landscape, any more than a list of choice words is a poem. The merit is in the design, not the material it is expressed in, and the best designs, like the best poems, make ordinary material significant by its arrangement. How many admirers could name the trees and shrubs at Versailles or Stowe?

A good designer can make a landscape—a whole series of different landscapes—by using the same dozen common plants. Thomas Whately said about the use of plants: "To be great it must be dull." This wise precept from the eighteenth century should serve as an awful warning to any designer tempted by mere frivolous variety. But it is meant for the producer, not for the consumer—it is in the making that a landscape must be dull, not in the finished design.

Nature's own methods are dull. However various and subtle the effects, nature's *methods* are large-scale, simple, and repetitive —and so must ours be to produce good landscape. Most of our designs, as Francis Bacon complained four centuries ago, are "too busie and full of Work." For it is dull to plant ten trees all the same instead of ten different ones, dull to lay out sweeps of uninterrupted grass large enough to reveal the land forms, dull to resist the fancy effects we are always tempted to try.

To control our misguided fancies we should assess our

If repetition is dull, then nature is dull.

The great avenue at Stowe—only dull to the planners.

landscape designs in winter, for summer is too generous, and distracts our judgement with vegetation beautiful in itself. But a good figure means good bones beneath the flesh, and in winter we see the chilly truth of our bare composition. If the massing and spacing are badly arranged, if the ground forms and general proportions are wrong, then in winter there is no disguising our fundamental mistakes.

For those of us who are distracted by the various charms of plants, there is a simple way to assess our designs—by photographing them in black and white, not colour. Distractions like flowers then become merely variations in the range of greys, and only the structure of the design registers. This is why so many gardens in photographs look depressingly like large salads (which is not of the slightest importance if the coloured reality pleases their owners).

PAPER PLANS

The greatest fault of landscape design is too much planning on paper. A plan is an intellectual abstraction, not a description of the visual landscape—unless we propose to live somehow suspended in mid-air. But we are not birds looking down on the scene from overhead. We do not see the landscape as a flat tray arranged with shapes, nor trees as darker circles on the grass, nor winding paths as elegant curves. We are ground-level animals looking along the landscape surface; we see in elevation, not plan; our trees have trunks and are outline shapes against sky, not grass; we have horizons and skylines, winding paths are foreshortened or lost; our ground is not a flat surface but rises and falls—a slight hill may block half the bird's-eye view, a single tree hide a mile-long vista. Perspective dominates our scenery.

Because we are all familiar with maps, we are used to translating elevation into plan, and anyone can draw a street plan on the back of an envelope. We are far less adept, however, at translating plan into elevation. Few of us could draw the streets from the diagram, nor, from a plan, have we any clear idea of what a landscape will look like. (And neither, so one suspects, have some landscape designers.)

"The Method commonly taken in this Affair [laying out a landscape] is that Gentlemen have their Ground survey'd, and perhaps the Levels taken, and then 'tis brought to London, where

Winter will only add to this flowerless garden by revealing the branch patterns of trees (North Andover, Mass.).

A summer garden which triumphs in black and white (Bodnant, Wales).

Too much going on in this drawing-board doodle.
"Too busie and full of Work,"
Francis Bacon would have described it.

there are a great many Drafts-men and Paper Engineers, so a
regular fine Scheme is made, and be it at never so much Disad-
vantage to the Nature of the Situation, or lead the Owner into never
so much Inconveniences, and needless expenses, it must be exe-
cuted." (Stephen Switzer.) Paper Engineers are, alas, almost as
common today as they were in the nineteenth century (when one
"ingenious Gentleman" marketed a kaleidoscope for designing
gardens in patterns of flowerbeds).

The way to avoid falling into the trap of paper abstractions
is to begin by looking at the site. Very few sites are ideal. Most
have a variety of good and bad features which must influence the
layout, and the first essential of all design is a detailed study of
these and of the vegetation of the area.

It is as important to assess dispassionately the site's good
and bad elements as to analyse exactly what its uses will be. These
are the fundamentals which all design should start from, and any
scheme is safely on the way to success if it provides for use while
mitigating the site's bad qualities and enhancing its good.

"The first thing then, in the Designing of any Works of this Kind, is for the Owner to get it surveyed, and to make Observations of all Hedge-Rows, Hills, Pits, Ponds, Woods, and all other remarkable Things within his Design, and also Remarkables without. By this he is furnish'd with all the natural Advantages and Beauty of a Place; but this is not quite enough yet; for he ought to walk over it, and view it over and over again, since there are many things that offer in the Nature of a Situation, that can't be contain'd in or thought of, upon a Plan; Such are the natural Advantages of Levels; Such are proper Places to sink Pits, or to raise Mounts, to view and diversifie the Prospect; Such are also proper Places to make Pond Heads, and to dig Ponds, and for the exterior Beauty of a Seat; Such are the Prospects of any noble Vale, Lawn, or surprizing Hills of Wood, and in short, any Prospect that is accounted valuable to these, there ought to be as open a View as possible." (Stephen Switzer.)

DESIGNING BY SPACES

Like architecture, like town planning, like most design in fact, landscape design is a composition of masses and spaces. The two great landscape styles of temperate Europe—which were transferred to America by the European settlers—both start from the basis of open space framed in woodland. Le Nôtre's classical seventeenth-century landscapes consist of open parterres and small separate gardens surrounded by trees and, leading out from these, the formal vistas cut through woodland.

Equally, the romantic landscape park of the eighteenth century is an open area in a belt of woodland, like a spacious forest glade, with water in the hollows, and separate trees or groups of trees modelling the internal space.

Both styles of composition, therefore, though so different in character and in their treatment of vegetation, are designed as spaces contained within masses; they are composed within the framework of deciduous woodland natural to the world zone of vegetation where they belong.

We experience masses from outside, spaces from inside. Our experience of space is thus different in kind from our experience of solids. A space contains us, it affects us directly and emotionally, we exist in its terms—free or constricting, reassuring or ominous, intimate or public. A prison cell is a space which contains us; so is a snug cottage. A space is our temporary environment. And so profound is its effect on our psyche that abnormal reactions can even produce nervous disorders, like claustrophobia and agoraphobia.

Land forms of hills and hollows, open areas with vegetation or buildings—these are the solids and voids which form the essential structure of any landscape. The fundamental character of a scene lies in how these solids and voids are balanced and grouped—hill or plain, woodland or open downs—and equally in how the varied masses and spaces of landscapes are consciously designed. The character of the eighteenth-century landscape park, for instance, is created by the particular arrangements of tree masses and open grass areas, and by their relationship to the wells and hollows of the land forms, including water; and this basic structure has survived two centuries (often of neglect) as an unmistakable landscape.

The same principles apply to the rural landscape. Certainly we think of the out-of-doors as open spaces, and so it is; but it is *spaces*—not merely open extent but definite three-dimensional volumes defined by solids. We remember openings in woods, for instance, lanes with hedges, fields in farmland—and these are all

A field is created by its enclosures—

A country lane by its hedges.

defined spaces. A field is a field because it has a boundary round it, and in England, where the hedges are disappearing with the new prairie farming, our dismay is by no means only at losing the vegetation of the hedgerows. For without hedges much farming countryside becomes incomprehensible: it has no structure and loses its human meaning when no longer divided into enclosures we can encompass and understand.

Woodland too, though by a reverse process, takes its identity from spaces enclosed within it. Solid woodland is anonymous, a repetitive pattern of trees where one mile is much like the next and the next. The distinctive places, the areas we remember, are the openings within the woods, the spaces defined by the trees.

Equally, in the consciously designed green environment the open spaces should be the essential areas of the design (the lawn of a garden, for instance), and the land forms and planting are the masses which define them. Just as a fine architectural façade is scant compensation for ill-shaped spaces either inside or out, so fine trees and shrubberies will have little value if the spaces they enclose are ill-proportioned or uneasy. Yet all too often outdoor spaces are scarcely considered; they are simply what happens between and around the solids. Seldom do planners now (the past

A landscape humanised by the farming structure of hedges and trees.

This prairie landscape is no longer comprehensible—it is merely extent.

was a different matter) begin with a layout of *spaces,* using buildings to define them; seldom indeed do landscape designers presume a uniform mass and create within it a composition of open spaces, vistas, paths, and so on, and then plant up the enclosing element. It is not a question of how much open space we want and how much vegetation. A design hollowed out of a solid can be made as open as we please; the question is which element we are primarily shaping. And unless we consciously create the space the positive will always be the mass. Mass is aggressive, solid, spreading; it will always look after itself. But space is tenuous, it leaks away, is easily fragmented, will not register unless we define it. Clearly in a combination of mass and void each will shape the other, but no matter how harmoniously they may complement each other one is nonetheless the positive. To design by spaces is also to design by function. It is the open areas of the landscape which we use and which therefore need laying out in usable shapes. In a forest climate a layout by spaces also makes ecological sense, for it means we base our design on the natural woodland landscape inherent in the area. Yet we seldom do this. We imagine a site as empty as the paper we are drawing on (and which of course it probably is), and we add the vegetation and other masses to a matrix of what we seem to presume will naturally be open space.

This means that in effect we are designing as if open grass were the natural state of the landscape. No wonder that maintenance is the problem it is, for in temperate lands it is not trees that we have to water but grass that we have to cut. And grass used as a matrix is sliced up into all kinds of shapes and sizes and meaningless snippets as awkward to mow as to use. For easy care grass areas need designing in simple shapes and in sizes suitable for machines, and the other vegetation should be used to provide an irregular matrix. It makes little difference to maintenance what shape a shrubbery or a group of trees is, but mowing a simple lawn surrounded by flowerbeds is an altogether different matter from mowing when flowerbeds are surrounded by lawn.

OPEN AND ENCLOSED SPACES

When we talk of space in landscape design we may mean either of two different kinds of space, which can be roughly classified as open or enclosed. Which category a space belongs to depends partly on the extent of the landscape and our relationship to it, but chiefly on the proportion between the space and the boundaries that define it. When the open area is large in relation to the height of the boundaries, this produces an open space. The third dimension is the sky, which, if limitlessly open above us, causes us to experience the space as a positive free extent. This is especially so if the area is on high ground. On the other hand, when the open area is small or the boundaries high, this creates an enclosed space, and we experience it in a completely different way: it is strongly three-dimensional, roofed by an implied plane between the boundaries, and we are within its volume. In an urban setting, to achieve the effect of enclosure the height of the surrounding mass should be at least a quarter of the distance across the space. In the country, however, where space and mass are more visible, a sense of enclosure can be given by a five-foot hedge round a small field (say four acres), though the same hedge round a forty-acre field would seem simply a fringe of vegetation. Thus when the surrounding masses are low, the open area may have to be smaller than slide-rule proportions would indicate if it is to keep its identity as an enclosure. This may be because of the sky—it seems closer to our earthbound level and is not merely an absence of enclosure but a positive emptiness which extends spaces into infinity.

These two different kinds of space have very different functions in landscape design. Open space is exhilarating, especially if it opens suddenly from a narrow enclosure. We are splendidly, soaringly free—birds of the air—and the sky is our element. The uninhibited, coming suddenly out onto the high expanse of Blackheath in London, have been known to fling up their arms and shout and run—like the dogs they bring with them.

Enclosed space is for different moods. It is a retreat to be sheltered and private in, to laze and recover in—or more mundanely, simply to escape the wind. In such enclosed spaces, sensations such as the scent of plants, the texture and slight movement of leaves in the trees, are heightened. It is important, therefore, to decide which kind of space we intend, and also (by no means as simple as it seems) which kind our design will produce. Have we planned an open space without considering whether high mass beyond the actual site (hills, high buildings) will change the proportions? Have we made it large enough to allow for the increasing height of vegetation, or will the sense of openness be lost as the planting grows up? Or equally will our snugly arranged enclosure disappear in overgrown green? And have we considered our enclosed space in

Open space defined by the roadside gardens and the low railing at the edge of the cliff.

Enclosed space with flanked view.

winter? Or will the sense of shelter leak away through leafless branches exactly when we most need it?

That our reaction to space is emotional and subjective we realize when we try to photograph it. Mass is simple to photograph (or would be if the camera discounted perspective as our eye does, and did not make high buildings lean together). But space is illusively difficult, for the camera only *sees,* it does not *experience.* It sees only gaps, extents, widely or closely grouped masses. To the camera space is not the positive experience it is for us.

DESIGNING WITH MASSES

There are various choices to be made about the plant material to be used as mass in the landscape. There is a choice of height and solidity, both visual and physical. There is variety of texture and shape, and of the effect of seasonal change. In a natural woodland landscape all the layers of vegetation are present, the herb layer, the shrub layer, and the tree layer. In design we have the choice of omitting one or more of these to achieve the different effects required. Mown grass, for instance, is the deliberate suppression of all the layers—flowers and shrubs and trees—to provide completely open spaces. Shrubs are mid-level mass; trees are high-level and can either be combined with the lower mass of shrubs or stand free in mown grass with the herb and shrub-level masses omitted. This deliberate omission of certain layers can be as telling a part of the design as the more obvious entirely open spaces, or the even more obvious placing of the positive masses. A vista between tree trunks beneath the high-level canopy of branches is a distinctive and beautiful landscape effect, and the dullest scene becomes interesting simply as a view.

Tall trees in grass also have the practical advantages of leaving the ground level free to walk on, and of being a very simple landscape to maintain by easy mowing. But though simple to achieve, the arrangement creates subtle and complicated effects of masses and spaces and vistas and light and shade.

The piloti structure of trees is invaluable in landscape composition. A deciduous tree is an overhead mass held above the ground on a trunk, like a pillar, so that a huge structure of leaves and branches causes no more than a narrow obstruction at ground level—an impressive achievement which engineers might well envy. A group of trees is like a building without walls—we can move

Regent's Park.

Trees and grass—simple and superlative (Green Park).

inside it, see out, see through it; we can use the space beneath for sitting, walking, outdoor living, even for building.

Trees in fact can provide voids within the masses of the composition, and no other landscape material can do this. Land forms, or other vegetation such as shrubs, will create wall-like enclosures, but only the piloti structure of trees provides spaces which are open at human level yet enclosed overhead. Other spaces created by trees are like the outdoor spaces created by buildings— open areas of grass defined by vegetation used as simple mass.

UNIFYING AND CONTROLLING ELEMENTS

Baudelaire's famous *"luxe, calme et volupté"* did not depend on material luxury but on *"ordre et beauté,"* and the beauty of order, of logically controlled design, is an intellectual satisfaction as valid for working as for luxury landscapes. It is the lucid ideal all landscape design should aim at whatever its function or character. A landscape needs a linking element which flows through the entire design and ties it together as a unified whole. The commonest way of doing this is with grass, and whether or not by conscious intent, smooth green lawns flowing through the whole composition create many pleasant gardens from otherwise uncoordinated bits and pieces. Grass has the same unifying effect as wall-to-wall carpeting throughout a house.

In nature a similar effect may be seen in whole meadows of buttercups, or a sweep of wild garlic, wood sorrel, even sometimes bluebells and wood anemones in woodland, or the uniformly brown fallen leaves on the bare floor of a beech forest.

In smaller areas, paving can tie a scene together if used as a simple all-over surface. This needs far more restraint ("To be great it must be dull") than is usual with most paper-pattern-happy designers, especially when tempted by the wide variety of concrete paving blocks. *In situ* concrete, which can be moulded to any shape, can unify a design better than stone slabs. Its plastic quality can create free-form shapes not possible with precast paving.

In larger landscapes ground surfacing is not enough, and the unifying element has to be higher and bolder. Hedges can coordinate a landscape at shrub level—as in the farming countryside and formal gardens—and on a still larger scale, belts of trees can create a boldly composed landscape of linked masses defining open spaces. There is no better form of unifying element in a suburban landscape than native forest trees. This is well illustrated by some of the suburban developments in northeast America where, even when the architecture is widely different, the woodland into which the development has been put links the units together into a whole.

Paths are also an important unifying element in the landscape—like roads, they interpret the landscape in terms of our passage through it, establishing a coherent progression through the area, even when we cannot see all the way to the end. Most important is the role of a path in composing and displaying the landscape. Paths invite. Even with no restrictions we generally follow them, and everyone who walks a path sees his surroundings in terms of it. It organises the sequence of closed and open areas, the sense of shelter and freedom, the arrangement of masses and spaces in the open perspective. Above all, a path fixes the viewpoints from which we experience the scene; it decides what we shall actually see or not see. If a path is well routed so that we follow it naturally, then the landscape is likely to be seen a hundred times more often

Belts of trees composing a large-scale distant landscape.

Urban landscape of high-branching equidistant trees, and grass used as moss layer. Omitting the intermediate layers (low trees, shrubs, and flowers) has produced the simple sophistication exactly right here with the smooth ground-shaping, curving rails, and parallel traffic lines (Park Lane, London).

Path leading the walker through an otherwise incomprehensible landscape.

from the path than from any other viewpoint. Although a path should be directional—otherwise it will not be followed—we expect natural obstacles, and paths can often be laid out to draw attention to objects of interest as well as exceptional views. (Capability Brown, the eighteenth-century landscape designer who laid out such gardens as Kew and Blenheim, according to one admirer, "was often very happy in creating these artificial obstructions.") Seats are traditionally placed on paths at points where it would be natural to pause. William Marshall, another eighteenth-century "improver," points out that "they are useful as places of rest and conversation and as guides to the points of view in which the beauties of the surrounding scene are disclosed. Every point of view should be marked with a seat, and speaking generally, no seat ought to appear but in some favourable point of view."

Management may also provide an important unifying effect. The beauty of a well-formed landscape lies in its logical order and consistent management techniques. The unifying effect, for ex-ample, of rows of poplars on the dikes in the Dutch landscape is

Path as route and sight line.

The seat defines the view.

made all the more effective by their uniform age and repetition. Our sense of beauty in order, logic, and fitness in our landscape is now probably better developed than our sense of beauty in wilderness. We have a strong functional or utilitarian attitude towards landscape and are depressed by the sight of abandoned fields. In the northeastern part of the United States the landscape is wilder, and abandoned farmland is common. The rural landscape has lost the unifying element of well-managed farmland. This is rapidly being replaced by second-growth forest, but during the intermediate stages the landscape is scruffy and depressing to European eyes.

DESIGN AND SCALE

In any composition there are three scales of design—foreground, middle ground, and background. (In landscape this is obvious, but it is equally true of other arts—architecture or dress designing or furnishing a room.) The background is the general composition, which should be clear, assured—and in good design, often simple. The foreground is the close-up detail—the texture of building materials, the weave of fabrics, the foliage in a landscape. This can be elaborately decorative without disturbing the simplicity of the general conception, since it is on too small a scale to register with the main composition. The middle distance is the difficult area (notoriously so in painting) and is where much otherwise good design goes wrong. It is essential that it should be right in terms of the overall concept because otherwise its scale is large enough to confuse and mar the main composition. In classic modern architecture the middle scale is commonly omitted: a beautifully proportioned overall design and superb close-up detailing, but no middle-distance decorative effects.

In the eighteenth-century landscaped park the middle-scale effects are deliberately suppressed: land forms are used, distant water, grouped forest trees, and after that grass—grass everywhere, from foreground to distance, and grazed to a uniform unobtrusive background. Not even the intermediate layers of the vegetation are used; no small trees, no shrubberies, certainly no flowers.

"Flower-beds hurt the eye by their littleness," said Horace Walpole, who deplored any "trumpery fragments of gardens" in the romantic green landscape. "We have returned to simplicity by force of refinement," is his succinct analysis of the landscape park

—"the utmost simplicity of cultivated order." It is why the English landscape, for all its professed imitation of nature, is so sophisticatedly different from any other.

The relationship of foreground and distance is especially important where the layout is to be seen chiefly from a single viewpoint, like a window. A small shrub in the foreground will overpower the largest tree in the distance, a nearby bed of tall flowers will blot out an acre of lawn. Even though we all know this is so, it is only with considerable practice that we can achieve the right balance in such a design. We are seldom conscious (though we can check by measuring on any photograph) what a very large area of distance is hidden by a very small area of foreground—a fact which is equally as useful for opening up desirable vistas in the view as for screening undesirable eyesores. However, this exact regulation of what we see is possible only from a fixed viewpoint. We can hide a gasometer or a telephone pole with a spray of roses only if we always look from the same rose-circled window.

THE FOURTH DIMENSION—TIME

Unlike architects, landscape architects are concerned with the design of a living entity. Plants grow and die, and, unless controlled, the landscape will be continuously changing towards the natural "climax" vegetation type. Most architects, understandably, are better at designing formal landscape than informal. They tend to use vegetation as if it were dead. They naturally think of it as an inert raw material like the others they work with and therefore use it to create extensions of architecture. Hedges are walls, grass is green surfacing, trees are static decorative masses. (They probably find vegetation most manageable as the cut-out green sponge they use to make models.)

But plants do not grow in the forms of architecture, nor are they precisely manageable in the way which formal design requires. Plants are not geometric but are subtly varying, many-dimensional structures in space. Smooth planes, symmetrical forms, and unvarying cross sections are as unnatural to plants as they are natural to architecture, and can be achieved only by rigidly clipping hedges, hard-pruning shrubs, and periodically amputating trees.

That these unnatural and expensive operations can produce excellent designs no one denies—or if they do they have only to visit Versailles, that superb statement of the glory of Renaissance man. But for living vegetation it is a form of torture much like Procrustes's bed, and in inexpert hands can produce the horrible mutilations which disfigure so much vegetation in our streets and parks.

Such designs are a form of organic architecture (at Versailles it even developed its own orders) constructed in material with a built-in and extremely inconvenient habit of growing (or dying). In such architectural-style design there is no feeling for plants as living entities. Yet a plant has its own inherent laws of development independent of anything we may intend, and designing with plants is like conducting a choir of animal voices—with sufficient labour and ill treatment they can be trained to make the special noises we want, but a far more reasonable way of controlling the chorus is to choose animals with suitable natural voices and simply let them sing (as Tudor huntsmen chose hounds by the pitch of their baying, so that a pack in full cry produced a harmonious chorus as they ran).

In vegetation this means choosing plants whose natural habits will produce the effect we want. Even so there are difficulties—such as the time it takes vegetation to grow to the necessary size. Architectural-style planting treats this interval as an unavoidable nuisance, and the design is for a static fully developed landscape. Therefore, the largest possible material is planted, encouraged to grow as fast as possible to the desired size, and from then on (since plants do not obligingly cease to grow at this arbitrary point) all further growth is cut back. It is significant that architects commonly specify evergreens—as nearly as possible they want the same effect all the year round.

This conception of plants as static material is by no means confined to architects, and is a perfectly understandable attitude. We are not, after all, accustomed to the raw material we are designing with having a life of its own, like Alice's croquet balls. But in the green environment nothing is static. The masses and spaces, the patterns and textures—the whole composition—are in a state of constant change. Landscape design is fluid four-dimensional planning with living material, with time as the fourth dimension.

Nor is time merely a matter of size, for at different stages of growth the design will also be different. Trees which when mature will form a leafy canopy with open vistas between the trunks will, when young, be low and bushy and block the view. Shrubs which when grown will define and enclose the spaces of the landscape will, when young, be merely low dots in the grass. Plants have distinctive patterns of growth which vary at different stages, and these should be designed for. A young tree is not an old tree in bonsai miniature but a differently constructed organism. A young cedar, for instance, grows in spirey Christmas-tree fashion, with no hint of the spreading horizontal planes of its maturity. In the perfect design all stages of growth would be equally attractive (as they often are in nature), but if this is unattainable by mere mortals, we should certainly plan for the developing stages of a design which may take fifty years to mature. In fact, most landscape needs a series of designs for the progressive development of the vegetation. The foundation is the long-term design which will survive for the future, but if only this were planted, the first generation of users could take little pleasure in the skimpy scene, nor would the plants be likely to thrive in isolation. Superimposed on this basic framework should be an intermediate planting design which will be at its best in the commissioner's lifetime (the landscape most generally considered), and since we are also impatient for immediate effect, these two compositions can be overplanted with fast-growing expendable vegetation to be removed as the longer-term planting develops. Such temporary planting has the advantage of quickly providing substitute vegetational mass, because the early effect of any planting is always unhappy—so many starveling trees and shrubs dotted about with no apparent relationship. It is only when the separate dots grow together into groups that the sea change happens and the design emerges. This takes so long to develop from the permanent planting that fast-growing temporary plants are a good idea to fill up the gaps and produce the essential grouping.

Therefore, we should always plan two consecutive landscape designs, ideally three. Likely intervals for most landscapes are roughly five, fifteen, and fifty years. These successive designs should be clearly conceived and a simple plan of maintenance worked out for the different stages, with instructions for removing outgrown vegetation. This should be explained to those who will look after the landscape so that they understand what is happening and what needs to be done to develop the design, though this type of programme is seldom carried through, and designs which depend on such constructive maintenance are likely to turn out very differently from anything their designers intended. It is quite common to see

Early planting as done in grass—

Grown together ten years later.

Layout of hillside terrace and windbreak for long-term development. No maintenance but periodic cutting out.

First five-year planting of expendable flowers and shrubs in gaps between permanent planting.

Eight years from layout. Herbaceous plants have gone; ground elder has taken over as ground cover and suppressed the grass; the permanent planting is growing well.

Twelve years from layout—the second stage ready for thinning. Close conditions have produced lush growth despite poor soil, exposed position, and no maintenance. With the permanent planting mass safely established the spaces of the design now need defining.

belts of mature pine—originally underplanted with beech—with the pine, which were planted as a nurse crop, having gradually smothered the beech. Compromise is generally essential, and when the landscape must develop unaided, a rough-and-ready method is simply to lay out the permanent design and infill it with plants which are naturally short-lived, and which will die of their own accord and be removed as the permanent planting grows up. And since most of the popular flowering trees and shrubs are also the shortest lived, everyone is happy—including next century's forest trees.

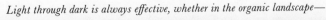

Light through dark is always effective, whether in the organic landscape—

LANDSCAPE AND HUMAN PERCEPTION

The human eye-brain combination is by no means a simple camera, but rather a subtly coordinated instrument for interpreting the world we live in to suit our human needs. What we see is not the momentary reality the camera records, but a human version of the scene created by the particular qualities of human vision combined with the relative values of the observer. The human eye judges relatively rather than absolutely; a grey which seems dark against a white background will seem light against a dark one, and a sunny area seen through trees makes both sunlight and dark trees more intense, light foliage against dark makes both more vivid, and so on. On the other hand, a gradual change from one state to another will level out contrast. Both effects can be used in landscape design—either to add contrast and variety to a dull scene or to play down an unwanted element.

The same adaptation of reality is applied by the human eye to size and scale. It exaggerates vertical dimensions and sees things as higher than they are. We may see hills, for instance, as a view of imposing heights and draw them as such in a sketch, but if we take a photograph of the same hills they will look tame

Or the built.

and low. Even a mountainous horizon may photograph as little more than an undulating plain. Equally in smaller-scale landscape our eye exaggerates the land forms, the height of trees, the changes of level, and so on, and if we are to produce the effect we want it is essential that the design should emphasise the horizontals in proportion to the verticals. This is especially important in ground-shaping, and most man-made land forms, though doubtless of excellent proportion in the scale design, in practice nearly always look too high for their extent.

Human vision seems naturally inclined to create enclosures in space even when the actual physical barriers are extremely slight, and given the merest suggestion of enclosure we ourselves supply the rest. A widely spaced row of lamp standards, for instance, arched over a road creates a continuous tunnel in space; half a dozen bollards will close off the side of a square for the eye as well as the motorcar.

This peculiar eye-brain propensity for creating continuous planes from slight indications probably exists because we are emotionally more comfortable in limited spaces enclosed from immensity (wishful seeing, in fact). We need defined and human-scale volumes which we can encompass and feel at home in, and only as a temporary exhilarating experience do we want to stand on mountaintops with nothing all round us, or sit on the empty sea in boats. For everyday living we need an enclosing home, a limited and defined territory, and even in public places like parks we seek out the partly enclosed as temporary territory—a space between trees, for instance, or a grassy bay among shrubs. Few people set up their deckchairs from choice in the middle of empty areas, and it is noticeable that most open spaces fill up first round the edges, which give some sense of enclosure.

OUTDOOR SCALE

Although we do not consciously change our standard of judgement when we leave a building, our mind nonetheless has a completely different sense of scale for indoors and outdoors. In the open everything is reduced, and what seems large in the indoor environment shrinks out-of-doors. It is why the foundations of houses always seem to enclose such ridiculously dollhouse-size rooms. A room is part of the indoor environment: we normally never judge it by outdoor scale—it shrinks to a fraction of its indoor

First comers establish their territory in bays round the edge—the open space only fills up later.

---

size when we see its outlines in the open. (It is no doubt this same effect in reverse which so disturbs people who fear spiders. Even large ones may be more or less tolerable in the garden, but as soon as they come in the house they are at once transformed into gigantic horrors.)

The design of architectural features for outdoors therefore needs to be deliberately on a larger scale. Proportions which may be excellent in a house seem small and fussy in a garden: paths need to be wider, steps shallower and broader. Planting designs must be simpler and bolder in large landscapes, whereas in small enclosed gardens they may be more complex and intricate.

The ways in which the eye may be deceived in its judgement of distance have always intrigued designers. As William Marshall wrote: "The narrower the vista the larger and more distinct the object. This appears to be a universal law in vision, and perhaps accounts for the extraordinary satisfaction which the eye receives from contracted views, and from the use of side screens in landscape."

The eye made deliberately uneasy. Drama created by the foreshortened upward view and heightened by the unexpected placing of the tree (Old Westbury Gardens, Long Island).

Shallow steps and the ornament, large scale for out-of-doors.

Because we mentally provide the plane which they indicate, these trees clearly define this awkward change of level. They separate the two spaces without creating a barrier. Circular beds in brick are right for the urban setting and (unlike grass banks) need no maintenance.

In an open landscape a structure seems farther away if the space between it and the spectator is not seen all at once but is broken up—for example, by banks of trees and shrubs. When we can see the intervening extent as a whole, then we underestimate the distance, as we do over water, but if parts of the ground are hidden, then our imagination adds extra extent to the areas out of sight, and the structure seems to be at a greater distance. (It is an effect we can often unhappily see in reverse when trees are felled.)

Vegetation can not only provide a screen, it can also act as a distancer, and can be deliberately used to make a structure seem farther off. It can also be used to increase the apparent extent of a limited landscape which, contrary to what we might expect, seems larger, not smaller, when broken up by added mass.

Landscape designers with too little space to achieve the effects they want have often been tempted to create them by trickery. False perspective was once popular for producing an effect of added distance, as by planting an avenue of trees which are smaller and closer together the farther away they get from the viewer. This is all very well as long as we do not know we are being tricked. But what when we do? And what if we walk down the avenue and look at it backwards? The only deliberate effects which really succeed are those which seem natural—such as planting the farthest-off areas in a design with small-leaved or dim-coloured vegetation (what Shenstone called "fadey" trees) to give an added effect of distance. The effect is heightened if large-leaved plants are used in the foreground, yet seen in reverse (the acid test) there is no offence, and to all but suspicious fellow practitioners of false perspective the plants seem chosen at random.

The eye is organised to present the brain with a working picture of the world its owner must survive in, and vision is therefore concentrated on those elements of the scene most likely to be useful. A frog's eye is blind to the finest view but acutely sensitive to the movement of flies. The human eye tends to ignore the obvious and concentrate on the less clearly seen. In a view we see the

A framed view immediately attracts our attention.

foreground as much less extensive than it really is in our actual field of vision (being close and comprehensible, it needs less attention), and the distance as much larger. This we can easily check by a photograph of the scene as recorded by the tiresomely impartial camera. It is why our early attempts to photograph towns come out as mostly road surface, and in landscape as foreground field, with the splendid view reduced to a mere wavy line on the horizon.

Distance reduces the true scale of what we see in a landscape far more than we generally realise, and in laying out an area with nothing to serve as scale it is therefore useful to have a supply of stakes whose height we know (two metres [about six feet] is a useful size) for judging the effects of distance.

There are other ways of achieving what is not so much deception as direction for the eye which can be used in landscape design without an accusation of trickery. A frame will always draw us to what is inside it, and our attention is thereby attracted to a view flanked by tree trunks, or to a gap in vegetation, like an opening in a wall. Land forms will also guide our sight line, as

A framed view immediately attracts our attention.
(A Woodland Landscape, *Jacob Van Ruisdael.*)

does water, and we naturally look along valleys, or hollows across level ground. Glades between trees and shrubs also create vistas our eyes will follow, whether the direction is solidly edged by vegetation or merely indicated by occasional planting. Above all, a path will focus our attention on whatever it leads to, both by clearly having an objective and by guiding our progress towards the view we can see ahead.

Even without a view beyond the site a focal point will draw our attention across the intervening area—a building perhaps, or even a seat, or simply a conspicuous tree or grouping of vegetation, especially if the colour contrasts with the background green. When subtler methods of providing emphasis or distraction fail, the introduction of screening may be the only answer. A structure in landscape is screened from view by any obstacle which interrupts the sight line between us and it, and however obvious this may seem, the implications are certainly not sufficiently made use of. For it means that obstacles varying in height from roughly that of the structure to that of the viewer can make equally effective screens—it entirely depends on their position along the sight line.

The farming inhabitants of old country cottages had enough of the out-of-doors in their working day—though these inward-looking cottages have much the same view as—

In screening a large element in the landscape, positioning is therefore all-important, since neither trees nor land forms (the likeliest obstacles) will be large enough to hide the element if they are—as they almost always are—near the source of the offence. The larger the structure and the smaller the obstacle, then the nearer the obstacle must be to the viewer; but also unfortunately the more static the viewer must be to keep the obstacle between eye and eyesore. In an open landscape with a free-ranging viewer this is a fairly insuperable difficulty, since complete screening means a continuous obstacle hiding all the landscape between viewer and structure. Of course there are landscapes so entirely unfortunate that we would rather be surrounded by trees and take claustrophobia as it comes, but often there is no need for such drastic measures. Most structures are not seen continually but only from limited viewpoints, or from stretches of road or footpath which happen to be aligned on them and thus direct our view. Often, therefore, a small amount of planting or landshaping in carefully worked-out proportions will screen the eyesore on most of the occasions we should otherwise see it. Sometimes no more may be

This modern house built for urban country-lovers.

needed than a short stretch of hedge or a slight rise of the ground planted with trees in the middle distance.

As we spend increasingly more of our time indoors the view from the window becomes increasingly important. In the old agricultural society ordinary people were not interested in views; workers spent most of the day in the open and were therefore glad to get indoors and shut off the outside world. Old country cottages are inward-looking, snug cells to shelter in; their windows are small and screened with curtains and forests of pot plants. Outdoor workers have more than enough of the outside world, and when the windows of country cottages are cleared of their lace and geraniums to look at the view—even more when picture windows replace old casements—then we know that the country workers have left and urban weekenders have taken over.

4.
The elements
of landscape-1

"It is difficult to explain on rational principles the existing form of the earth's surface, yet how interesting is the subject to those who inhabit it." So said William Marshall, and the existing form of the earth's surface, unexplained or not, is clearly the basis of any landscape and will be a controlling factor of the design.

LAND FORMS, WATER, AND STRUCTURES

Probably man's earliest additions to the landscape were land forms, and it is astonishing how long they have endured. Mounds, protective earthworks, tumuli, and barrows are enduring evidences of our remote past, and they survive because they are relatively indestructible; ditches may fill with surface litter, exposed surfaces will erode with weather, but where soil is shaped and covered with a fleece of vegetation it is more stable than anything else we build—which should certainly be an argument for the use of landshaping in landscape design. Walls may fall down, vegetation comes and goes, but land forms survive without maintenance and despite vandalism or any other of the woes our landscape flesh is heir to.

Landshaping, if done at the right stage in a project, is cheap compared with most other landscape operations—certainly cheap if we include, as we must, its subsequent protection and maintenance. It is in fact one of the very few landscape operations in which one ever hears that the cost was less than expected. The classic example of this is the Guinness hills at Park Royal London, where the saving in transport costs for disposing of waste material from a nearby underpass financed the entire landscape work on the Guinness project, including the consultant's fees.

One reason for the relative economy of landshaping is that it makes use of our vast new machines and sources of power. We have only to watch the splendid new earth-shaping dragons at work to realise that with the right machines at the right moment (as we often have when laying out new landscapes) a hill here and a hollow there are swift and easy creations compared with the laborious and vulnerable results of much other landscape work.

In designing from scratch, the cut and fill of earth-moving can often be organised to balance out; computers do the calculations for vast works like motorways, but for smaller-scale designs a model with mouldable putty is invaluable for ensuring that all the material you take from one place ends up in another. When there is no material, enterprising designers have been known to invite free dumping of subsoil, thus producing mass for shaping and topsoiling.

Landshaping is also fast—a matter of days, not years as planting is—and for many effects we want in a hurry, a screen, or a windbreak, for instance, this is a powerful advantage. A ten-foot bank can be produced in a morning, but a ten-foot hedge may take ten years to grow, and if the bank is planted with shrubs the effect is not likely to be very different. It actually may be an improvement, since the choice of plants is wider for the bank, and the hedge is likely to grow thin at the bottom, where it matters. Another important consideration is that earth banks help cut down on noise. And despite what is commonly believed, vegetation has very little effect as a sound barrier except psychologically (we tend to be less bothered by noise when we cannot see its origin).

But apart from such practical matters our feeling for nature, like that of the eighteenth century, is for the rough rather than the smooth. "If the ground be very unequal, 'tis a great Charge and a very gross Vanity to level it. For there is a Kind of Beauty and a Sure Refreshment in a Wilderness. The most beautiful Gardens may be made where the Ground is the most irregular and uneven, where there are Hills and Pits: these unlevel spots dictate to Men of Taste those Varieties, which by discreet Management will afford the greatest Beauties to a Garden." (Richard Bradley.)

Certainly a site of irregular land forms starts with many advantages to modern taste, especially if the slopes are varied and to a large extent reciprocal—as are the sides of a valley, or mounded ground with a level underlying base. Such hilly sites can suggest their own landscape, the land forms holding a varied composition harmoniously together. A single uniform slope falling all one way is a different matter. It may overlook an attractive view, like the classic Italian gardens, in which case it can be organised as a series of viewpoints for looking at the prospect, and the view itself will

We all like the land forms of the chalk country (Berkshire Downs).

But man-made land forms are something else (Stoke-on-Trent).

coordinate the landscape of the slope. But if such a slope has a building on it there are problems which arise concerning the views from the windows of the building in addition to the practical difficulties of providing the necessary areas for use. The windows which look along the fall of the slope will frame the diagonals of the land surface, and this, seen against the horizontals and verticals of the window openings, produces the uneasy effect of sliding downhill. The remedies are either to level enough ground to check the slope or to mask the line of the land surface with planting.

Indeed, on any uneven site there are various visual effects which will influence the design. A slope seen from below, for instance, will not seem steep, but from a facing hill will appear precipitous. Straight lines on rolling ground will look like flowing curves, as field hedges do in the country; equally, curves may be lost at eye level, and so on. It is essential to think of an uneven landscape from all viewpoints, examining the site with care, sometimes even making a scale model.

There are also the peculiarities of human vision to allow for, since we do not always see the world objectively but in terms of what we need for our existence in it. This functional vision, as we might call it, affects the way we see slopes. Our life is not altered by what slopes look like but by whether they make movement difficult. An empty landscape of hills and valleys might seem one of easy flowing contours until the vertical of a walking figure or the tipped plane of a car appears to jolt the eye to the reality of steepness.

"It is only by a pleasing illusion that we can imitate Nature's bolder effects," wrote Humphrey Repton. But the pleasing illusion needs very careful handling to imitate even the least bold of nature's effects. And though landshaping may create forms indistinguishable from nature's, it can also produce hills like mudpies and hollows like scooped-out ice cream.

In landshaping there are two essentials: first, to produce land forms appropriate to those natural in the area; and second, to blend them discreetly into the existing landscape. Appropriate shapes should as far as possible imitate what is there already, always remembering the eye's inbuilt exaggeration of vertical dimensions. If it is to seem natural, any man-made land form will need to cover a far larger area and to be much lower than we expect, for our man-made shapes are nearly always too small and too steep and too sudden. They all too often remind us of tip (garbage) heaps.

The level terraces and hedges break the cross fall of the land beyond, which would otherwise disturb the horizontals of the house and make an uneasy side-slipping view from the windows (Delaware).

The wood edge is a straight line, but landscape is three-dimensional.

The flattened Z outline of spoil heaps.

Regraded spoil heaps (Stoke-on-Trent).

S curve of well-shaped bank round a car-park (Longwood Gardens, Del.).

Crudely shaped road verge—in rounded land forms.

Vegetation creating the effect of a valley on near-level ground (Kew).

Planting to heighten a shallow bank between park and city traffic (Regent's Park).

"So great is the power of trees of correcting monotony, that, by their means, even a dead flat may become highly interesting." (Uvedale Price.)

Landshaping for new housing. Revealed by mown grass, the land forms are a small-scale version of the surrounding landscape (Connecticut).

They are also in general too regular. Natural land forms have been modelled through eons of weathering by water and wind. Their shapes are not symmetrical, nor their slopes uniform, and to imitate nature we must replace wind and water by cunning and bulldozers. The junction between hill and plain, for instance, is not a simple sudden change from slope to level; nor is a man-made bank a simple shape like a chamfered wall. The sharp edges are weathered, the acute hollows filled in. A cross section of a natural bank is not a flattened version of the Z but of the S. Even the crudest cuttings will weather to this natural profile in time—but since not in our time, they need our help.

"In Nature inequalities are usually well blended together; all lines of separation have, in the course of time, been filled up and therefore when in made ground they are left open, that ground appears artificial. The connection is, perhaps, the principal consideration. A swell which wants it is but a heap; a hollow but a hole; and both appear artificial: the one seems placed upon a surface to which it does not belong; the other dug into it." (Thomas Whately.)

Bearing in mind Whately's warning, we should beware of indiscriminately creating hills and hollows where before there was an apt and harmonious evenness. The effect of the receding planes of a level landscape, with groups of trees distancing hazily one behind the other, is supremely beautiful, especially in a misty climate. Moreover, flat land is far less vulnerable to intrusions, which are so much easier to screen when the angle of vision is acute.

PLANTING TO ENHANCE LAND FORM

In natural landscape irregular ground levels tend to be lost, since vegetation grows taller in the shelter and deeper soil of hollows than on exposed higher ground. On ground which is only slightly irregular, therefore, all changes of level may disappear under a cover of natural vegetation such as woodland. In landscape design one way to create an effect of varied levels in a basically flat area is to plant slight rises of ground with shrubs and trees, keeping lower areas as short grass. This produces a convincing illusion of hollows between rising banks. Nor is it really an illusion: we have simply substituted vegetation for land mass. For this it is essential to use shrubs which are dense at ground level and preferably thickened by evergreens, so that the true land surface is lost and we visually accept the rising shrubs as rising ground. Trees alone will not create this effect, since we still see the flat ground beneath them.

A fine example of planting to enhance natural contours can be seen on the chalk downland of parts of England where closely grouped clumps of beech, planted mostly in the eighteenth century as positive landscape features, emphasise sweeping contours and form visual focal points on the skyline. Another example of this type of planting is the knots of pine trees often seen on sandy hills and ridges.

Very gentle land forms, either natural or man-made, can be exaggerated by the kind of planting which has been described, or their subtlety can be fully exploited by the use of grass. Grass is a positive element in the landscape, an important part of the design material of any scene we create, and we should use it consciously for positive effects. It is sympathetic both in texture and in colour, and when the light is low, or on contoured land, or when there is short grass combined with trees, it produces beautiful soft-edged shadows. The eighteenth-century designers used land forms, grass, and trees almost exclusively to achieve their romantic "painters'" landscapes, linking them to the swells and hollows of the surrounding countryside. Though our needs may be different from theirs, we can learn much from studying their methods.

WATER AS A LANDSCAPE ELEMENT

"Water," said Thomas Whately, "though not absolutely necessary to a beautiful composition, yet occurs so often, and is so capital a feature, that it is always regretted when wanting; and no large place can be supposed, a little spot can hardly be imagined, in which it may not be agreeable; it accommodates itself to every situation; it is the most interesting object in a landscape, and the happiest circumstance in a retired recess; captivates the eye at a distance, invites approach, and is delightful when near; it refreshes an open exposure; it animates a shade; cheers the dreariness of a waste, and enriches the most crowded view; in form, in style, and in extent, may be made equal to the greatest compositions, or adapted to the least; it may spread in a calm expanse to soothe the tranquility of a peaceful scene; or hurrying along a devious course, add splendour to a gay, and extravagance to a romantic situation."

There scarcely seems anything further to say in praise of water, but Whately continues with a whole chapter on whether

Nothing like water—even in a concrete gulley.

rivers should be widened to lakes, how to site bridges for picturesque effect, on the use of cliffs and hanging woods to add to the wildness of romantic shorelines, and other equally unexpected advice—essential no doubt for the ambitious eighteenth-century designers but needed too in our utilitarian age, which could, if it had a mind to, use its prosperity to create romantic scenery.

Increasingly large areas of water are created for reservoirs and such, or old mineral workings and quarries are flooded for amenity use. These large areas are mainly functional, however, and the site, shape, and extent are chiefly determined by practical consideration. While they can provide exciting features if carefully treated, we cannot always choose where they will be, and the design is mostly concerned with the niceties of their composition in the landscape. The land forms of the water edge can be altered to produce a more attractive shoreline, recreation may need special waterside arrangements, and shoreline planting can greatly enhance both the water and its relationship to the landscape. And since water is a magnet which holds our attention, any area with water

Not a country lake but a city reservoir. Water landscapes are inward-looking and self-contained.

can be developed as a self-centred landscape indifferent to what lies beyond. Even in a setting of depressingly ugly scenery we can make a complete oasis—we have only to screen the outward views, and they cease to exist for anyone in the water landscape.

On a smaller scale the use of heavy plastic waterproof liners has made possible the creation of pools and even lakes in places where they were seldom possible before. Such pools are generally shallow, but this is of no importance, since it is the surface of the water we see, not its bed, particularly if the lining is black or coated with mud. Only by measuring can we tell if a lake is five feet deep or fifty. A drawback of shallow water is that it may fill up with vegetation, especially if the lining is covered with soil for protection. In nature, shallow water is rarely permanent, for where vegetation can root and reach the surface, its yearly dying down and regrowth gradually change the water to marsh and in time to dry land. The Broads in East Anglia are rapidly shrinking because this process is now going unchecked, as are many areas of marsh and swamp in northeast America. Shallow water in general needs regular cleaning.

New techniques make man-made pools as manoeuverable as any other landscape element, but they are nonetheless convincing only if they lie in natural hollows of the ground and the surrounding land forms are shaped to make them seem natural.

WATER'S INTRINSIC QUALITIES

Water, specifically, among the elements used in landscape design, has its own intrinsic qualities. For one thing the locality has to be considered. In hot and arid lands we want fountains, falling water, the sound and sense of water as a longed-for relief from the parching air. The spray, the coolness, and even the thought of water in dry heat are delicious; but what when the air is already humid and the summers wet? Forest climates are not short of water, and it is easy to see why the best use of fountains and moving water is not in Britain or northeast America but in California and southern Europe. In temperate climates the use of still water, of gleaming levels, pools and lakes—and on a more lavish scale than arid regions can ever dream of—is where design can excel.

The movement of water is always fascinating, whether in flowing streams, cascading waterfalls, or the ripples of a gently

Shoreline shaping and planting of man-made lake (Kew).

Four feet of water as convincing as forty. Paddling was evidently thought of as large scale for out-of-doors (Kew).

Shallow pool filling up with vegetation. Unless cleared, this will soon be dry land (Bucks Common, Gerrard's Cross).

Man-made pool in carefully shaped land forms (private garden, in Connecticut).

The shine and patterns of water.

Jets used only to keep the surface of the water in motion (Steuben Glass building, New York).

Stream becomes lake by damming, landshaping, and lavish planting. A linear water garden on a narrow strip of land through a new town centre. Stream and garden would scarcely have registered if treated in the usual way with mown grass banks (Hemel Hempstead).

Building and setting mutually adapted (Arcadia, Stowe).

disturbed surface. The surface of any water is seldom still, and its effects are fascinatingly various—a brilliant sparkle when shattered by light wind, soft spreading rings from a single disturbance like a stone or a fish, ripple patterns from moving objects like water birds swimming, or water lovers boating. Even in a confined space which breaks up the patterns, the surface of all but the stillest water is an ever-moving dapple of light—perhaps enchantingly reflected on the ceiling of a room, if the pool can be sited beneath the window. Fountains are sometimes best used as gently gurgling springs just disturbing the surface of the water to keep it in motion.

The sound of water is endlessly attractive, splashing, lapping, liquidly plopping—its sound is as varied and as various as its motion. Even the surface tension of water has been appreciated—perhaps it still is—by the Japanese, who filled shallow bowls full to overflowing to admire the elastic level of water above the rim. Certainly calm water has its own hypnotic attraction, especially on a large scale. For here is the perfect serenity of the perfect horizontal, the intellectual conviction of absolute rest. The lagoons and canals of Venice are the beauty of the city, not only because of their watery qualities, or for the contrast between their simple surfaces and the rich splendour of the architecture, but also because the water provides a ubiquitous and perfectly level base from which the masses of the buildings rise in serene balanced verticals.

But water is a precious element in any landscape—not only the kind of unique environment that Venice provides—and the design should therefore emphasise its unique qualities. Except to naturalise banks it is a great waste to fill a water area with vegetation—with lilies and bog plants, which, however attractive in themselves, make the water merely another sort of flowerbed. We have plenty of space on land for all the flowers we want, but there is seldom as much water as we would like. Flowers for water are therefore a poor exchange.

STRUCTURES AS A LANDSCAPE ELEMENT

"The materials of natural landscape are ground, wood and water," said Humphrey Repton. To which he added, "Man adds buildings and adapts them to the scene." And so man may have done in the halcyon age Repton was writing of, when Arcadian temples were added to landscapes simply as decorative eye catchers. However, not everyone admired them: "Half the number would be twice too many," said Horace Walpole of the temples at Stowe, and Capability Brown's famous park was originally stuffed with such a plethora of temples that it might almost have counted as a built-up area. "Art has evidently done too much at Stowe," said William Marshall disapprovingly. "It is over-wooded and over-built: everything appears to be sacrificed to Temples." But then Marshall had moral and scientific objections as well as aesthetic, and considered temples a species of useless ornament, still more offensive, because more costly, than the other comparatively innocent eye traps. "Whether they be dedicated to Bacchus, Venus, Priapus, or any other genius of debauchery, they are, in this age, enlightened with regard to theological and scientific knowledge, equally absurd." (The "comparatively innocent eye traps" were such things as "a barn dressed up in the habit of a country church, or a farm-house figuring away in the fierceness of a castle, or a painted steeple daubed upon a board and stuck up in a wood.")

Today we are rarely concerned with the use of structures in the landscape for such frivolous purposes as eye traps. However, the principles of siting a large building in the landscape are in some ways similar to those of siting buildings in the eighteenth-

An eighteenth-century house sympathetically sited in existing land forms with minimum reshaping (Creech Grange Dorset).

century landscape. Certainly there may be views which we wish to screen but also views to which we wish to draw the eye. Unfortunately, it is rare that we wish to draw attention to new buildings, for the people who build our modern landscapes are seldom noble aesthetes but factory builders, spoil-heap pilers, housing-estate developers, motorway makers, and all the intractable rest. Nor is there any "scene" as Repton meant it—a controlled and consciously designed landscape. Nor are most of our modern structures added: they are fundamental; and their land use dominates—though without integrating—the landscape. To say they are not adapted to the scene is the mildest understatement for describing their general complete incongruity both to the landscape and to each other.

SITING STRUCTURES IN THE LANDSCAPE

As a visual element in the design, a building is a mass of a certain shape and colour and texture, and takes its place with other masses such as land forms, vegetation, and any other existing development. Buildings in parks, power stations in the countryside,

Terrace, level lawn, formal paths, and hedges unite the building with the site (Holland House).

factories in grounds, schools in playing fields—many large modern
buildings are separate structures in an open space. In such settings
the building is only an incident in the general scene, and, therefore, its first importance is usually not in itself but in its relationship
to the whole. The new structure in fact exists in terms of its context,
but whatever architects may profess in theory, in practice they all
too often design buildings in a visual vacuum. Their concern with
the setting often seems to be no more than the site plan, and their
first working sketches are commonly of the building itself, not of
its place in the scene it is part of, which they rough in only as
an afterthought. Even final drawings are often of a building as
separate as an egg, generally from an inaccessible viewpoint, and
often casually decorated with full-grown but nonexistent forest trees
added *à choix*.

The difficulty of setting a building in its site to fit in with
scenery around it was recognised by Uvedale Price: "It is an easy
matter to make out such a design as may look well upon paper;
but to unite with correct design, such a disposition as will accord,
not only with the general character of the scenery, but with the

Factory disguised as stately house (Bliss tweed mills, Chipping Norton).

particular spot and the objects immediately round it, and which will present from a number of points, a variety of well combined parts—requires very different, and very superior abilities."

First sketches, therefore, should be of the general scene, showing the land forms, the broad composition of masses and spaces, and any trees and existing structures. The new building at this stage should be no more than an amorphous presence responsive to its setting. There could even be a dozen sketches of a dozen slightly different arrangements which would suggest twelve subtly different buildings. For the most important thing—certainly in an open setting—about any building from the Parthenon to a cowshed is its relationship to its site.

THE ROLE OF PLANTING

Many industrial buildings such as power stations, oil refineries, and large factories are so enormous they cannot do else but dominate the area, and their relationship to the landscape can only be on a comparable scale. Planting on the site is usually completely inadequate and should concern itself with the screening of small-scale messiness in as simple and unobtrusive a way as possible. The link to the general landscape and to the human scale must be made with trees, which redefine the buildings in a way we are used to. Indeed we unconsciously use trees as our measure in judging size out-of-doors. The tree which shelters us from the sun may be a towering giant many times our size, yet in detail it is in our own human scale of perfection—twigs and buds and leaves and flowers belong closely and intimately to our personal range. The same tree which in the open landscape can compose with a massive power station can also give us a spray of leaves for a jar on our desk.

It is not only the incompatible size of industrial structures that disturbs, but also the incompatible scale. We use the words "size" and "scale" as if they were synonymous, but they are by no means the same thing. The scale of a structure is in the size and proportions of the units of which it is composed: the size of a structure is simply how much there is of it. Thus, though we may feel emotionally overwhelmed by inhumanly large masses, a difference in size is perfectly comprehensible—it is simply the difference between a brick and a pile of bricks. It does not make us mentally uneasy. A difference of scale, on the other hand, does. Incompatible

The vast scale of our new industrial structures in the countryside. Only the horizontal mass of a belt of trees could compose these huge towers in the landscape—

As it does at the Exxon refinery on Southampton waters.

scale in the same composition produces a particularly uneasy sense of mental disturbance—it is, in fact, one of the most telling visual ways of suggesting madness.

It is indisputable that in the varied range of modern structures there is also a varied range of scale—scale tends to vary with size, and a cooling tower, for example, is different both in size and in scale from a house. This is probably one of the fundamental reasons why the postindustrial built environment shows little sign

Albrecht Dürer: scale and size and madness.

---

1. Mixed cups and saucers. But it is the intellectual concept of scale which makes them wrong, not their size or proportions.
2. See them as candlestick and plant holder and we are happy.

yet of fusing to a comfortable whole, as the built environment did in the past, no matter how mediocre the separate buildings, or how unlikely they were as neighbours. They were not only much the same size but—more important—on a similar scale.

Here again vegetation can help to compose the landscapes we live in, because all vegetation, whatever its size, is of a more or less uniform scale. A tree is on the same scale as the flower growing beneath it—its leaves and blossoms are of similar size; the

Not many people's idea of home. But at least trees have been planted between the house and the madly incongruous stacks, and when four times their shown height they should help— if only as distractions.

tree is merely larger. Given a landscape with structures of disparate scale as well as size, generous planting, especially of trees, will go far to compose it to a compatible whole, both by linking the varying sizes and also by establishing a uniform natural scale which overrides the built disparities.

In less temperate climates, the local natural vegetation is often not desirable for the living areas. In southern California, for instance, the contrast between the desert flora and the lush green in the man-made living areas is marked. The built environment in these places has no relevance to the local habitat; it simply rejects it and substitutes conditions more acceptable to the people who live there.

In a temperate climate, however, the built and the natural environment share the same conditions, and the trees of our living areas can be the local trees of the surrounding countryside invited in to keep us company. To a large extent the same trees will grow in every kind of landscape—living areas, industrial estates, parks and gardens, rural countryside, wild areas—and this is our great good fortune. For it means that our many different land uses can take place in a single diversified setting integrated by the same vegetation; trees and people can live harmoniously together in the same conditions to create a harmonious landscape.

This can never be achieved where amenity planting—whether through climate or design—is fundamentally different from the local vegetation. Yet we often choose to ignore this great advantage of our climate by deliberately planting different trees for different land uses—for living areas, for country roads, for industrial districts, and so on. We even use non-native trees for screening—though their alien presence chiefly serves to proclaim the eyesore we want to forget. By thus emphasising the various and often haphazard land use of an area we create a jigsaw of unrelated pieces, when by planting the same local trees for all types of land use we could keep an intrinsic unity in our scenery.

ROADS

Buildings are not the only intruders that have to be considered in design. Roads in their various guises are all structures in the landscape. The old network of roads and lanes is getting

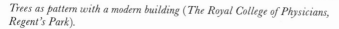

Trees as pattern with a modern building (The Royal College of Physicians, Regent's Park).

eroded away by overuse, but as the great new motorways relieve the pressure this process may possibly be arrested and some of the lovely country lanes with all their zigzag bends, flowery verges, and leafy tunnels left undisturbed. The fact that the new fast roads had special design requirements was fortunately recognised early in their development, and in Britain, mainly as a result of the Landscape Advisory Service set up by the Ministry of Transport, many of the new motorways set an example of good landscape design. Hopefully this will inspire those concerned with other types of roads, which, although they need equally skilful treatment, have different roles to play in our motoring lives.

While routing and geometric design play a major part in the success or failure of the fast trunk roads and motorways, or indeed of any road, the planting is of very great importance and must be conceived both in the context of the high-speed vision and safety of the users as well as the off-the-road lives and safety of its neighbours. And despite all the problems inherent in planting on disturbed soil near traffic, and with sight lines to consider, if the planting is right and relates with the land masses this will decide finally whether it has that look of inevitability and logicality which pleases from both on and off the road.

It is in the controlled progression of the linear landscape of a road that the designer's skill must be used. The design should not only create variety and interest, but could by its character indicate the different regions the road passes through. With sensitive consideration of the land forms and by the types of trees planted

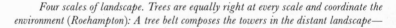

Four scales of landscape. Trees are equally right at every scale and coordinate the environment (Roehampton): A tree belt composes the towers in the distant landscape—

As does a single tree in close-up.

The same tree unites the tower block and the inhabitants—

as well as the views which would be concealed or revealed, the remoteness we feel on a motorway could be translated, even at the high speeds we travel, into a feeling of awareness of the natural regions of the countryside. This would be a far better way to spend public money than by doubtless well-meaning but often inappropriate planting.

And is the right size for human beings—even the smallest.

COLOUR IN THE LANDSCAPE

The colour of structures is a subject which has provoked a lot of controversy, and the work done by the British Council of Industrial Design has helped solve some of the disputes. This work attributes colour to three coordinates, hue, value (light reflection), and chroma (intensity of colour). The recommendation of the advisory panel was not to choose colour to match the landscape, because a mismatch is inevitable in the countryside's changing colours. (The use of green as an attempt to camouflage buildings usually fails.) Instead it is recommended that an adjacent hue be chosen, giving compatibility rather than an attempted match.

John Piper, speaking at a conference of the Council for the Protection of Rural England, concluded that the only satisfactory colour to use in the countryside is black, pointing out that if shiny it reflects light and thus has a greater range of tone than any other colour, and if matt it is as black as black when in shadow and in sunshine it changes tone completely (giving the same kind of variety of tones which occur in hedgerows or tree groups). This seems excellent advice—to which might be added the idea of compulsory khaki for tents and caravans, where camouflage seems the only answer.

5.
The elements
of landscape-II

VEGETATION

Vegetation was Humphrey Repton's second category of landscape material. Important obviously for its basic function within the ecosystem, it is also in many ways the most adaptable and readily available of the materials. With it we can define space, give shelter both visual and physical, and form a framework in which to live our lives, linking urban, industrial, and agricultural regions with a matrix of our own choosing.

By what and where we plant, and by the way we control its growth, we can create the character of our landscapes. For not only should our planting please the eye and suit the soil and climate, but skilfully contrived it can give identity to meaningless areas. The *genius loci* consulted by the eighteenth-century romantics may seem to have little relevance for us, but could we not persuade new plants to inhabit our industrial and urban landscapes? To achieve this we must plant now, lavishly and everywhere. Mainly trees, proper trees, not garden treelets like laburnums and cherries which cannot be included in the same category as our native oak and beech. In any case there will always be plenty of cherries, for their popularity is unassailable. It is the forest trees we need to be concerned about.

We make endless excuses for not replanting—that trees cause accidents, disrupt roads and footpaths, undermine foundations, crack walls, and so on. Nothing is easier than to find excuses for what we do not want to do, yet we have only to look around us to see trees growing everywhere, close against walls, or set in pavements, with no ill effects. Of course trees can cause trouble; poplars in clay, for instance, are notoriously liable to drain and shrink the subsoil and disturb foundations. They need watching and removing if necessary. But even where no hazards exist we still do not plant.

Even when they have got space they don't plant trees—excellent landshaping, acres of mown lawn, and three shaveling cherries! What this site needs is hundreds of trees to make a barrier between the living area and the thunderously busy main road.

This sterile expanse could at least be planted in a row of trees to separate houses from traffic and soften the bleak environment.

A disastrous layout, which could explode with leafy green.

PLANTING TREES

"It is in the arrangement and management of trees that great art of improvement consists. Earth is too cumbrous and lumpish for man to contend much with, and when worked upon, its effects are flat and dead like its nature. But trees, detaching themselves at once from the surface, and rising boldly into the air, have a more lively and more immediate effect on the eye; they alone form a canopy over us, and a varied frame to all other objects, which they improve. In beauty, they not only far excel everything of inanimate nature, but their beauty is complete and perfect in itself; while that of almost every object requires their assistance." (Uvedale Price.)

If trees were so essential for designers with the lavish resources of the seventeenth- and eighteenth-century aristocracy, they certainly are for us. "Those that would appear splendidly frugal should plant trees." So Stephen Switzer advised eighteenth-century landowners dismayed at the cost of formal gardens, because trees planted by forestry methods, or as three-foot whips in grass, are cheap both to plant and to maintain. Cheaper than grass, in fact, to plant—and certainly to maintain. (Check local prices to assure yourself just how true this is.) Forest transplants are small

Although this treeless space is a larger area—

This tree-filled well is less claustrophobic as well as less soul-destroying.

and need time to make an effect but they establish themselves quickly and grow fast. Prices for standard trees are considerably higher (as is the cost of laying turf instead of waiting for grass seed to grow). It is instructive and surprising to work out comparative costs for a given area maintained as woodland or as mown grass. The initial planting cost even of standard trees can be offset in a matter of ten years or so if compared with the costs of a similar area sown and maintained in grass.

"Variety of Uniformities makes compleat Beauty." So said Sir Christopher Wren, and in all the arts variations on a theme are universally satisfying. Wren was concerned with restraint in architecture, not in tree planting, but his maxim is even truer of trees. To enjoy variety there is no need to plant an indiscriminate mixture of species which will never compose to a coherent landscape, since in a single species of tree there is endless variety.

Grown in the open with light all round, trees take on different forms from those grown in woodland. Instead of developing tall trunks to raise them above competition they spread sideways into the space and light, and a tree in an open field occupies all the vegetation layers from ground level to treetop. The same tree in a closely planted group will grow tall and taper with a long clean trunk and a platform of branches at canopy level. Or grown among bushes in a hedge, it will be of intermediate form with a trunk to carry it clear of the hedge, with a dome of branches above. In a group, a tree will develop on one side only, in an exposed position be wind-pruned and leaning, and so on. There is also the variety of age—young trees are of different habit from old ones, sometimes of different foliage.

There is also the variety of grouping, since a group is not simply a number of separate units, but becomes an entity, often growing into the shape of a single enormous wide-spreading tree. A group of the same kind of trees growing together will provide Wren's "Variety of Uniformities," because, depending on whether it is at the edge or in the centre, exposed to wind or sheltered, on the north or south of the group, every tree, although of the same species, will be distinct and different.

"No group of trees can be natural in which the plants are studiously placed at equal distance, however irregular their forms. Those pleasing combinations of trees which we admire in forest scenery will often be found to consist of forked trees or at least of trees placed so near each other that the branches intermix, and by a natural effort of vegetation the stems of the trees themselves are forced from the perpendicular direction which is always observable in trees planted at regular distances from each other. No groups will therefore appear natural unless two or more trees are planted very near each other (sometimes in the same hole) whilst the perfection of a group consists in the combination of trees of different age, size, and character." (Humphrey Repton.)

We too seldom attempt this kind of planting. Certainly it would mean there could be no once-and-for-all layout, since the groups would have to be thinned and some replanting done every five or ten years. But this method would enable greater continuity of effect in the overall design, which is not possible with single-age equidistant planting. It would mean that there would always be young growth in the mixed population, and young trees, like young people, have their own particular attractions. They are not merely incomplete adults, but young creatures at a distinctive and charming stage of their development, with their eager vigorous growth, the pliancy of their half-formed wood like the pliant bones of children, and a gaiety almost like that of young people.

PRESERVING EXISTING TREES

Where trees already exist on sites to be developed they should be guarded from all the hazards of site works, bonfires, dumping machinery, and the perilous rest. Certainly they are murderous villains who write specifications beginning with "Clear the site," for they are signing an indiscriminate death warrant for every tree and shrub in the area. Such blind destruction is folly even on purely mercenary grounds, and wise developers are learning to value trees as profitable assets on any site, rooted treasure whose presence may decide the plan of a sensitive layout.

Here again, as so often, America has the leafy advantage over England—though this does not mean that she necessarily realises or profits by it, or keeps the trees she has in the places where most needed. For though eastern America is lavishly wooded, and early development was mostly houses on spacious lots that were generally kept as woodland, yet much recent higher-density housing is often treeless, and the scene is as bleak and bald as anything in England.

Nonetheless, development in the northeastern United States often starts with clearing woodland, whereas in Britain trees that

Clear-the-site development in what was almost certainly woodland (New York suburbs).

New housing laid out between existing trees.

The same housing on a cleared site.

do exist may be protected by Tree Preservation Orders in areas which care to apply them, making it an offence to fell them, imposing fines on offenders, and insisting on replacement planting. This is excellent but limited, for preserving existing trees is like furnishing our houses with antiques—fine if they are there and we can afford them; but most of our working furniture will have to be new. Since there are not enough trees, we sometimes cherish them with tree surgery and the rest, but eventually they grow old and die. On sites being developed, old trees are especially at risk, for even with the most enlightened protection, arrangement of levels, avoidance of root disturbance, and so on, mature trees are not as adaptable as young ones, and the changed condition of essentials like water supply, root run, and so on is likely to shorten their lives. Young trees should therefore be planted to develop in the new conditions and eventually to replace the older ones. All too often the charm of a scene depends on trees which are clearly approaching the end of their life, yet there is no sign of so much as a single young tree planted to follow on. The primary purpose

Instant maturity with Tree Preservation Orders. This well-established garden for new housing was a raw building site a month before the picture was taken. Cautious landshaping over old roots, turfed lawns, trees, and shrubs carefully preserved through the building operations and filled in with new planting (London).

of any "tree preservation" legislation must be to ensure the re-planting of young stock rather than to preserve trees in a state of decay.

INSTANT TREES

"My present and sole occupation is planting, in which I have made great progress, and talk very learnedly with the nursery-men. . . . The deliberation with which trees grow is extremely inconvenient to my natural impatience. I lament living in such a barbarous age, when we are come to so little perfection in gardening; I am persuaded that a hundred and fifty years hence it will be as common to move oaks a hundred and fifty years old as it is now to transplant tulip roots. I have even begun a panegyric or treatise on the great discoveries made by posterity in all arts and sciences." (Horace Walpole.)

Now, two hundred years later, though we have made only

doubtful discoveries in the matter, our modern impatient science-can-do-anything age tends to think of fully grown trees as being as easily available as geraniums whenever we want them.

But this is not so. To begin with, where are the thousands of trees to come from in our increasingly treeless landscape? They are simply not there, and even if they were, the difficulties of removal are serious. Instant trees are wishful thinking, and the new machines which are to perform this arboreal removal operation are in effect simply huge trowels which cut through the roots and scoop out the tree with a trowelful of soil round the base of the trunk. Such rough-and-ready no-preparation methods may suit the machine, but they certainly do not suit the trees. With intensive aftercare and drastic cutting out of branches to balance the lost roots these trees may survive, but they seldom flourish. And many that do not die instantly, die slowly. Nonetheless, when young trees would otherwise be destroyed in site-clearing the operation is certainly worthwhile. Then the trees should first be "banked" in a sheltered environment where they can grow new roots close to the trunk and thus have much more chance of surviving the final move (or they can die unnoticed).

It is possible, of course, to move semimature trees successfully (as gardeners have done for centuries), and where the old methods of preparation and of keeping an intact root ball are used they are commonly successful, especially if combined with the new techniques for preventing water loss and so on. The trees still need such care as watering in dry seasons, especially in low-rainfall areas—and it is important to remember that even the seventeenth-century royal designers with unlimited labour found "continual waterings a very great Slavery and Expense." Nor do the trees always recover completely from the removal. It is often some years before the trees grow any larger, and growth may be permanently stunted. It is surprising in fact that trees ever do survive transplanting, since this can never happen in nature. Cold, drought, sometimes fire, being broken or even eaten—these we might expect a tree to adapt to, but not to being transplanted. Fortunately for us, most young trees are resilient, but in middle age it is a major and often disabling operation. It is planting not in terms of the tree's life but of our human impatience. "Begin betimes with trees and do what you list; but if you let them grow great and stubborn, you must do as the tree list. They will not bend but break, nor be moved without danger." (Cecil Gordon Lawson.)

Underground car-park in a London square. The developers
may think that these trees are all right—

But the trees know better.

Since a landscape architect was employed, some new planes have been planted. Three in this picture.

Trees well protected during new building operations (Cambridge, Mass.).

Certainly don't cut down the tree, but why not realign the wall? (Cambridge, Mass.).

The benefits of moving semimature trees are obvious—we have trees from the start. Being large, they are less vulnerable to damage in busy places, and though seldom used for this purpose, they are excellent for nursing up young trees to take their place. They are, however, extremely expensive, and we should be very clear exactly why we need them and use them only then. The usual reason is to create an immediate effect, and for this they are the only solution. But there are also reasons we need trees ten, twenty, fifty years from now—and these are not best fulfilled by semimature trees, in terms of either cost or tree development. Young trees planted where they are to grow permanently are far better provision for the future (even for the near future). If semimature trees seem the answer for a certain site, it is far wiser to buy only half as many as wanted and to spend the rest (probably less) in planting a hundred young ones among them. In far shorter time than most people suppose, the young trees will overtake the old and will develop into more vigorous and shapely specimens, from which we can choose those we want to keep and gradually cut out the rest (probably the original large ones).

DECIDUOUS TREES

A particular virtue of a temperate climate which we seldom realize is that most of our trees are deciduous and lose their leaves for the winter. Deciduous trees are rare both in time and in place, for the earlier floras which covered the earth were chiefly evergreen, and even in our present flora, deciduous forest is a relatively narrow band of vegetation between the evergreen conifers to the north and the Mediterranean-type evergreen trees and shrubs to the south. Deciduous trees are an adaptation to a temperate climate, for it is after all an extraordinarily prodigal way of life for a tree to shed the entire mass of its foliage every autumn and regrow it every spring. It is a vast effort to make every year (in comparison, the stag's horns are trivial) and must impose a huge strain on the tree. It is certainly not surprising that the world's longest-lived trees are less lavish of their energies and are evergreen.

Thus the astonishing beauty of winter branch patterns—the vital structure of the growing organism—is a treasure we owe to our climate. So are the fragile dying graces of autumn, and the miraculous explosion of spring foliage, with every leaf new and young and filmy, and no messy background of the old and tired

This multiman operation followed several years of preparation.

Semimature trees with new council housing. The best of intentions, but only the sycamore is happy: the rest are languishing or dead. Half the number (all sycamores) interplanted with young trees and shrubs would cost less, produce a better immediate effect and far better final trees. It would also hide the ugly stays (three per tree) and save endless man hours mowing grass in the cat's cradle of trunks and wires (London).

as there is with evergreens. Our deciduous springs would seem an incredible miracle if we knew only tropical evergreens and northern conifers. We have only to plant a deciduous tree, and with no effort from us it will provide a year-long succession of changing effects, each as beautiful as the last. As William Shenstone writes, "Trees have a circumstance that suits our taste, and that is annual variety."

Treasure at a more practical level in the built environment is a tree's convenient change of mass with the changing light. In summer, when a tree is solid with leaves, it casts a heavy shade, but because the sun is high and shadows therefore short the shade falls chiefly in a pool beneath the tree, and not on nearby windows. And in winter, when the sun is low and shadows long, the same tree's shade will lie on nearby buildings, but since the leaves have fallen the tree is no more than a thin trellis of bare branches patterning the light, and does not darken the windows. We can then plant deciduous trees far more freely and closely in our living areas than we ever could winter-thick evergreens.

Deciduous trees with houses. Evergreens would reduce this sunny winter scene to gloom (Nash's Park Village West, London).

CONIFERS

The virtues of conifers are on the whole less suited to the built environment, certainly of towns. The fact that they are ever-green not only makes them too gloomy in winter for planting near buildings but also means they are intolerant of pollution, since they do not shed their accumulation of urban dirt as often as do decidu-ous trees. For example, in the woodlands established to mitigate the industrial areas of the German Ruhr, dying conifers languish among the luxuriantly healthy deciduous trees. Nor do most coni-fers grow with the clear trunks that create usable spaces below their overhead mass—essential in high-use areas—though this is not true of the pines, which when adult develop an open-branching head and picturesque habit. Also many pines have attractively coloured and textured bark, and with the unique soft bunchiness of their long-needled foliage it is easy to see why Chinese and Japanese gardeners prize them.

In the general landscape the drawback of conifers is their structure. In America with its very varied flora there is no problem,

The high canopy of pines. Market laid out beneath group of existing pines (Hemel Hempstead).

since conifers occur naturally in the mixed woodlands, especially in the early stages of regrowth to forest, but in Britain, except for the Scotch pine and the shrubby yew and juniper, conifers are not native. Most introduced conifers are rigidly symmetrical in structure both in outline and in detail, either solid columns and cones of green or trees with uncompromisingly pointed tops and regular branch patterns, very difficult to group together, and much disliked en masse in forestry planting. Combined with deciduous trees, however, conifers can make good groups for parks and gardens, and they can provide high-level evergreen mass—a function which may be so important that it outweighs any disadvantages. How else, for instance, can we provide a year-round barrier of high vegetation? Or thicken small groups of trees to keep them solid in winter? Many conifers, in what for them are our luxuriant summer-forest conditions, are very fast-growing—a great enhancement of their virtues in our impatient affairs. And their dark foliage can produce interesting combinations of green when grouped with other vegetation. The looser conifers, like yews and the larger-spreading junipers, are particularly valuable for low- and middle-height planting. Above

A mixture of deciduous trees and evergreen shrubs screens buildings beyond.

all, the texture of conifers is unique—a deep pile like rough velvet. Only conifers provide that particular dense furriness which can compose so well both with the summer leaves of deciduous trees and with their winter branches.

SHRUBS

Broad-leaved evergreens share some of the virtues of conifers, such as year-round mass and green life in winter, but in a climate with frost in winter they are mostly shrubs (the evergreen oak is a slow-growing beautiful exception). Mixed groups of evergreen shrubs and deciduous trees make a well-balanced solidly based composition and are particularly attractive in winter.

Since a plant, like a building, is also the space it occupies, the effect of shrubs in the landscape is very different from that of trees. Shrubs occupy the same level in space as we do ourselves, both the same space on the ground and the same eye-level space. Human beings in fact are shrub-layer height. Surrounded by shrubs of eye level or higher, we can neither move nor see, and shrubs therefore

Between the foreground grass and the background trees is a busy road and two rows of parked cars. Even in winter the traffic is lost behind the belt of shrubs (Hyde Park).

The cars here are at much the same distance, but with no eye-level planting they dominate even in summer. (No one on the seat and no wonder—the forward view is equally undisguised cars.)

are far more claustrophobic than trees. Trees and herbs, however solid their mass, are not on our own level; we can see either over or under them, move either between them or on them, as on grass and between trees. Thus, though the mass of a tree in the landscape may be many times that of a shrub, its effect upon us may be less—certainly when close—and this is why a tree when felled and lying at our level looks astonishingly larger than it did when standing. It is also why free-growing shrubs in the space we share with them often need more room than we allow them in our designs.

The shrubberies the Victorians left us now seem oppressive and gloomy, too big for the villas they envelop. But the value of large-scale shrub planting for screening low-down clutter and, used with trees, for shelter against dust, noise, and wind is enormous both practically and from a design aspect. In screening structures in open landscape, as well as in the many types of maintained rural landscape which we are increasingly finding need for, the planting must be with groupings of indigenous plants or with such introductions as have become accepted as near nature. The vegetation should not intrude either by incongruity or by overemphasis.

Shrub planting in urban areas, considered in detail in the next chapter, can have greater latitude as to species. Its functions and maintenance will be different, and it should have harmony with the architecture both in detail and in form.

In these as in all planting situations it should be remembered that in the outdoor landscape the number of visual patterns we can follow at once is limited and that the most satisfying effects are achieved with simple contrasts on a scale fitting to the site. Form, colour, texture, and shape are characteristic features of the material used, and indiscriminate mixtures cancel each other out like the music of a fairground, or two radios playing together. When the mixture is not indiscriminate some of the subtlest and most satisfying effects are produced by combinations of plants with different growth patterns which enhance each other like the super-imposed themes of contrapuntal music.

Grass used only to keep open space in the landscape needs far less maintenance than for its other two functions, though be-

Long grass and wild flowers in June—but everyone must keep to the path,
where the grass is cut.

cause its function has not been clearly thought out it is often kept mown far more closely than it need be. Here the essential is to prevent high growth, not to provide smooth surfaces, and therefore only occasional cutting is necessary. Where feasible, grazing provides excellent control, as in the eighteenth-century landscape parks, but this is seldom practical. We think of grass as a material, not as separate plants—as grass, not grasses. Yet the plants which make up an area of long grass are as much entities in their own right as the shrubs which make up a hedge (and which equally lose their identity when aligned and clipped and become merely "hedge"). Long summer grasses swaying with wild flowers are one of the most beautiful of all close-up landscapes—lavish and intimate and various—and will grow as free and flowery in designed landscapes as in old-fashioned meadows (well-farmed modern meadows do not contain flowers).

This sight is rare, however, except on road verges, where fortunately economy seems to be spreading, and verges which were once mown down to featureless green strips for miles together are now left high all summer and waving with wild flowers. In most

Why grass instead of vegetation? And if it must be grass, why put the bollards where they make mowing as difficult as possible?

public places long grass is not practicable, since we take it for granted that grass can be walked on. We are not used to grass but to *mown* grass—a different man-made ground cover resistant to trampling. The fact that grass happens to be longer than usual makes no difference—we walk on it just the same (if only to pick the flowers). And areas of long grass and wild flowers are no more resistant to trampling than herbaceous borders. They *are* herbaceous borders—wild ones—and if we treat them as walking areas the result is as unhappy as any trampled flowerbed.

Since grassland is not natural to a temperate landscape, and grass areas depend on maintenance, their management needs planning. In the old days of hand scything, an area of any shape or size could be mown with equal ease (and with equal labour), but this is not so in our modern machine age, and just as farms must now be laid out for easy machine working, so must landscape—especially the grassy spaces. Two small lawns will always take longer to mow than one twice the size. And if the grass is an awkward shape, or much broken up, it will take more time and fray more tempers than a very much larger single expanse.

A clear case for plastic lawn bought by the yard and fitted like carpet—hard-wearing, drip-dry, and no nonsense about mowing the impossible slopes and angles. Plastic-haters might prefer green gravel periodically sprayed with weed killer, but they would find the banks a problem.

FLOWERS

Flowers are the last and least important class of vegetation for design, even though millions of contented gardeners consider them the essential raison d'être of the whole process.

We may well feel with John Rea that flowers are "the wealth, glory and delight of a garden." We often feel the same about the pictures and personal treasures in our houses. But we must first have a house to put them in, and equally we must have a garden for flowers. Just as architects are concerned with the structure of buildings, so landscape designers are concerned with the structure of landscape. When considering the overall design, flowers are largely irrelevant, for we can no more make a good garden by starting with flowers than a house by starting with the ornaments on the shelves.

In northeast America the climate tends to discourage both gardeners and flowers: the summers are too hot and the winters too cold (for many of our English favourites at any rate). There is no long season, as there is in England, of lavish uninterrupted floweriness from early spring to late autumn when plants from all over the world are comfortably at home in our mild ocean weather. It is significant that American gardens are so often of better design than the flowery English ones—there is more consciousness of structure and grouping, better use of trees, shrubs, and ground cover. One begins to question whether concern with flowers may not mean unconcern with design.

At a landscape distance, flowers are different from leaves only because they are a different colour. And because they provide only scattered dots rather than whole areas of colour, they are apt to make the same visual impression as litter. Roses as usually planted are particularly unhappy landscape elements; separate bushes in beds of bare soil display to perfection their fallen and rotting petals. There are exceptions. Drifts of daffodils under trees are lavishly beautiful in spring, as are sheets of crocuses in grass. Seeds sown in the bare earth of new areas of planting flower lavishly during the second and subsequent years, and gradually die out as the planting grows up. On the sandy loess in Germany, for instance, lupins cover hundreds of acres of land reshaped after mining, turning whole hillsides misty blue between the sapling poplars, binding the soil, forming humus, and fixing free nitrogen.

Even the flowers of trees and shrubs are a pleasure added

*Flowerbeds not registering as setting for a factory—but probably no one wants
to distract attention from this splendid 1930s period piece.*

Nonetheless trees make a better composition with the unregarded side elevation.

Parks departments tend to think in terms of flowers, but flowers are not the ideal vegetation for roundabouts, especially since no one gets close enough to see them except motorists busy with their driving.

Rose beds don't make good elements for landscape composition (Regent's Park).

Daffodils and cherry in early spring.

rather than being basic to design. Flowers are best as separate entities and seen in close-up; we value them for themselves, not as landscape material. They are most suitable for small enclosures in parks and gardens, for window boxes, and sometimes for plant containers; for flowers, like faces, are interesting only when we come close enough to see them in detail. It is odd that we should be so strongly attracted by flowers, since they are designed for insects, not for us. It is for their flowering stages nonetheless that we value many plants, though it is important to remember that they are only a temporary kind of decoration. They provide no structure in themselves but need a permanent framework, which should still be satisfying when the flowers have gone.

GRASS

In landscape, grass has three main functions, and any area of grass may fulfill any one or more of these. First, grass may be used as part of the visual design, and grown and tended as lawn

Flowers are for living with (London mews).

*Flowers for a living-room terrace, grown in containers and replaced as they go out of season.
Here yellow autumn chrysanthemums with autumn leaves (Delaware).*

The early New Towns had a grass fixation. Why these shorn acres except to keep mowers in work?

Sunken underpass in New York's Central Park. A fraction of the maintenance as well as the space, and many times more attractive.

A "carpet lawn" as foil for free-growing vegetation.

for its own sake. In England a fine lawn is the chief pride of many gardeners, and in many gardens the most important feature. A "carpet lawn," as gardeners used to call it, is valued for its exquisite velvet texture and its uniform smooth surface, which provides an enhancing foil for other vegetation. Grass is used as a moss layer, since grass does not naturally grow in this smooth close-cropped way, and it has a very distinctive character. The lawn itself is deliberately laid out as part of the design. In any landscape it produces an effect of the consciously designed and carefully tended, and is why, for instance, remote Swiss hillsides, closely grazed round clumps of trees and shrubs, have such an unexpectedly parklike and genteel air.

The second function of grass in landscape design is as ground cover in utility areas. As living ground cover, grass will withstand more wear than any other. This function may coincide with the first—lawns are for use as well as for looking at—but not always. The grass cover of games areas is valued for its practical qualities, because it provides a sympathetic organic surface. This is its down-to-earth role when used in places like English football "pitches," or American football "fields." On golf courses, grass is as important for part of the landscaping as it is for the fairway, and is consciously used thus by the landscape architects who lay out the proliferating and often excellently scenic golf courses in America.

The third function of grass is to preserve open space in the landscape, for vegetation reduced to grass is well below the critical height that makes the difference between open and closed spaces. This function may combine with the other two functions, because visual open spaces may also be open areas we use, but this is not necessarily so. We may, for example, want open vistas in a landscape simply to see beyond the encircling vegetation, or we may, more practically, use grass verges along roads to keep the sight lines open.

6.
The built landscape

Although the natural habitat may be the foundation of our landscape, it is no longer the setting of our urban lives, certainly not in Britain. Here most of us are not conscious that we live in the forest zone and that our natural landscape is woodland. For the actual landscape most of us inhabit is urban and has been for generations, and for generations before that it was the man-made pattern of farmland. Most of us are centuries away from anything approaching the natural habitat, and the privileged elite responsible for landscape design in the past were even more thoroughly insulated. They were leaders of fashion, and since the Renaissance, Western fashion has been consciously urban. And if the background of landscape designers is urban society, then the attitude of society to natural scenery will be part of the designers' attitude to landscape—as indeed it has been ever since landscape design has had conscious styles.

HISTORICAL BACKGROUND

The first designed landscapes in Britain were gardens—small enclosures against the hostile world, with the surrounding barriers the chief element in the design. Within these outdoor rooms favourite plants were grown (often wild flowers), though with no particular order. It was enough that flowers and people were safe together in a tiny haven in a vast and unkind world. Nature was feared.

These are the gardens of medieval paintings, and as society grew more prosperous and the world less perilous the gardens grew larger and more confident. But the main theme was still enclosure, and the design was still dominated by the surrounding walls and moats and hedges. Man's consciousness was closely contained within the garden wall and the world outside ignored.

The first big change came with the Renaissance, when a newly confident society felt for the first time that man was master of his environment: landscape design lost its fear and set its sights on the horizon. Like the Renaissance, landscape began in Italy— with the formal gardens of the Italian villas—and later spread north to France, where it changed and expanded under Le Nôtre, whose landscapes were imitated all over the world. The Renaissance garden was a formal composition of the utmost self-confidence, and its dominating vistas proceeded with superb assurance into the landscape beyond. Man's intellect was supreme, and nature was subdued.

Man, however, is a restless and changeable creature, and by the eighteenth century, this very subjection of the nature he once feared began to pall. The fashion was a return to "Nature" as idealised by the painters Claude Lorrain and Nicolas Poussin, and it was expressed almost to perfection in the eighteenth-century English landscape parks. The intricacies and mysteries of Nature were admired by a sophisticated society which equally idealised the Noble Savage. That it seems to us now an elegantly classical Arcadia is due partly to our earthier twentieth-century version of nature (every society has a different conception), but also to the fact that most parks we know are by Capability Brown, whose style, among the varied substyles of the eighteenth-century landscapists, was known as the "Serene," and indeed was criticised as unnaturally genteel and insipid by admirers of the more rugged landscapes of the "Sublime" and the "Picturesque."

"Your system of levelling and trimming and chipping and docking and dumping and polishing and cropping and shaving destroys all the beautiful intricacies of natural luxuriances," said Patrick O'Prism to Marmaduke Milestone in Thomas Peacock's *Headlong Hall*. However, compared with the Renaissance formal garden, the landscape park was a very real return to nature and was conceived in terms of the natural forest habitat of its country of origin. It was also the last true landscape style in Europe, a current which ran out in the nineteenth-century shallows of the gardenesque, the neoclassical, the plant-grower's garden, and the carpet bedding that still survives in parks and popular taste.

THE CHARACTER OF THE BUILT LANDSCAPE

In landscape as so far considered the organic elements have been predominant. The scene has been composed of natural material, perhaps with widely varying proportions of built structures but always with the bulk of the landscape material organic. The buildings—whatever their functional importance—have been visually only a small part of the scene. This is not true of the present landscape of towns and cities—nor even of the close-grouped villages of the past. Here the scene is composed of buildings and other man-made structures, to which vegetation may or may not be added. When it is, it is incidental, not structural, as in the landscapes so far discussed. In such a fabricated landscape, the buildings are no longer separate masses in the composition but the actual material from which the environment is constructed. This makes it a landscape fundamentally different from anything considered up to now, and the principles of its design are also different, for buildings have to be considered as an essential part of the scene.

In an environment in which architecture plays so important a part, architects should clearly be the best people to design the whole. But the kind of architect that is needed is not, as Uvedale Price says, "a mere builder," but rather "one who has studied landscape as well as architecture, and who feels that each different situation requires a different disposition of the several parts." Too

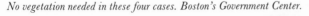

No vegetation needed in these four cases. Boston's Government Center.

St. Martin's in the Fields.

Airy hilltop village.

Airy rooftop walk, like cliffs above a river. Buildings as sculpture (South Bank, London).

often architects tend to concentrate on the buildings, and the spaces between them—the urban landscape—are often either misdesigned or ignored.

Architecture concerns the defining by masses of both the indoor and the outdoor spaces we inhabit. A space is a positive entity, and in towns the shapes and proportions of the open areas often make more impact on us than do the buildings which bound them. A street is a channel we move through, not two rows of buildings. A square is a formal enclosure, not four façades set at right angles. These urban spaces, when confidently human in scale, can give great visual and intellectual satisfaction. Vegetation, with its urgent organic patterns, may only disturb the balanced geometry, and leafy trees blot out the harmonious perspectives. In the effortlessly urban townscapes of the Mediterranean, for instance, vegetation is for shade or for occasional decoration: the quintessentially human scene is created by buildings. Georgian townscapes too were often entirely architectural compositions, and the original eighteenth-century squares were treeless—urbanely assured man-made settings for a sociable town life. They needed no trees to humanise them or to decorate their elegant façades. Nature was limited to sky and people and perhaps a little low greenery strictly disciplined by its setting.

Even country villages are often almost without vegetation. There is plenty of green in the surrounding countryside without overgrowing the man-created habitat of firm dry surfaces and humanised masses and spaces. Any vegetation is kept in its place—a narrow row of flowers along the angle of a wall, shrubs pruned to topiary shapes, trees lopped or pollarded and no question of nature taking over. Often a village's best combination of green and built is a contrasting view of the countryside at the end of a close-housed street.

VEGETATION IN THE BUILT LANDSCAPE

It is true that a built environment without vegetation presupposes a confidently humanised quality in building that we seldom now seem to achieve in our townscapes. Perhaps it is no longer widely achievable with the inhuman scale and function of modern city structures. Could the eighteenth century have composed a harmonious scene of tower blocks and walkers, motorways and houses? Even their original squares now need trees to veil the

Large trees stuffed into narrow spaces between buildings—enriching the urban texture without weakening the urban structure (St. Paul's Cathedral, London).

alien alterations we have made to them. It was the late eighteenth-
and nineteenth-century developers who planted the London squares
with trees, and who also began the process of destruction and
botching that we have continued so enthusiastically since. The trees
are now imperative: they are the chief (sometimes the only) beauty
of many of the squares, coordinating the patchy and incongruous
additions by their dominant natural structure.

Vegetation in towns should be fitted in—almost never made
room for. The best urban planting is often crammed in as an extra:
it is "as well as," not "instead of." It decorates the city scene without
destroying the city character. But the built environment without
planting needs a quality of design that is rarely achieved in modern
townscapes. Too often it is necessary to use vegetation to create
spaces, a function which should be adequately performed by
buildings in an urban setting.

IN AND OUT PLANTING

"One day I realized that the whole of a landscape architect's
raw material—when the city architect and city engineer and traffic
manager have done their stuff—is nothing but Sloip. (Space left
over in planning). Actually I wasn't regretting it, just saying that,
in a city, landscape architecture is the poetry of odds and ends."
(Peter Shepheard.)

In the built-up urban landscape there are two completely
separate categories of open space. One is these odds and ends of
urban Sloip; the other is parks and gardens. It is not simply a
question of size: these are essentially different types of open space,
their function and use is different, so is their place in the city
landscape, and so therefore should be their design.

The "poetical" odds and ends, the bits and pieces of urban
landscape, are an integral part of the city's architectural fabric,
to be landscaped as part of the urban experience. Parks and gardens, on the other hand, are not part of the city environment: they
are separate landscapes, contained within their boundaries. Parks
are not incidental to the city's layout as are the bits and pieces;
they are planned for an allotted space, deliberately created alternative environments inserted into the city's fabric in the way we
might set aside a room in a house to make a conservatory. The
planting in these two settings has different functions and needs very
different qualities. It can for convenience be called OUT planting

In *planting: then (Winchester)*—

And now (high-density housing, in London).

and IN planting. OUT planting is the landscaping of any open area and has already been discussed. It is vegetation used as a setting for buildings, as part of the low-density landscape, or to create a green outdoor environment. This is planting in terms of the vegetation itself, and in built-up urban areas it applies to parks and to a lesser extent to gardens. IN planting is the vegetation of urban spaces and is planting relative to the architecture which is the structural material of the scene.

The design of parks and gardens starts from premises completely different from those of the design of small urban spaces and thus needs a completely different approach. Yet all too often any open space, no matter how small, is treated in the same way, and what should be distinctively urban places are laid out as miniature gardens. That these are unlikely to succeed is evident. Gardens are enclosures, cherished and vulnerable, preferably private, certainly unsuited to the hard use of busy public places. Small areas of grass will not stand the concentrated wear, flowerbeds are either too easily trampled by crowded walkers or else restrict the use of the

Embarras de railings. Railed in for gardens—but why? And where are the gardens? This should be free-access open space, with plants in paving and sit-on-me seats, not keep-out railings.

area, and fenced-in paths through snippets of grass and miniature flowerbeds all enclosed in a setting of large buildings are out of character and out of scale with the surroundings. Urban spaces may be green oases as leafy as any garden, but they do not have the separateness essential to gardens. Such landscape is not created from organic materials, but is part of the built-up town fabric where organic elements are additional. Even though the vegetation may be dominant, the structure of urban spaces should always be architectural.

Plants must exist on architectural terms not only in that they suit the design and the spaces available, but in that they can survive the unnatural conditions of root run, depth of soil, water supply, amount of light or pollution, and so on. And it should never be overdone. A town should be first and essentially a town; and though in existing close-built towns the risk of too much green is slight, since we do not pull down valuable buildings to make space for vegetation, in new development—in Britain, anyway—indiscriminate enthusiasm for green is a very real danger. For

Perhaps they had *to use up the railings, but why not at least plant a tree and some shrubs inside?*

It is difficult to see what could be less suitable than grass between these facing slabs of flats, railed off and not even for sitting on.

How not to treat a potentially attractive square. No trees, no shrubs, no flowers, no sitter on the seat—no wonder.

The reductio ad absurdum of the garden in cities. Stone wall, parapet, lawn, and flowerbed in the space for a single plane tree.

despite the unresolved struggle with the aggressive motorcar, towns and cities are primarily for walkers—they are the one environment where legs are still the most efficient form of transport. Large spaces are antiwalker, and to explode towns with green creates a non-pedestrian environment. Even trees are bought at the high price of loss of close city character.

Landscape is sometimes divided into the "hard" and the "soft." The hard includes roads, buildings, paths, walls, paved areas, and so on, and in an urban setting should form the structure of the landscape defining the spaces. The soft landscaping is the planting. The relative importance of hard and soft elements in the landscape changes as the landscape becomes more urban. Whereas it should hardly ever be necessary in urban areas to use vegetation as a structural element in the landscape it may well be so in suburban areas.

SCALE AND SIZE

The size and shape and proportions of small urban spaces are determined by the existing structures. Any design should take into account the fundamental difference between scale and size.

Whatever the size of the area, and it may be very small, it is nonetheless an outdoor environment, and as part of the out-of-doors the design must be generous in scale. It must compose with tall buildings, wide roads, open sky—the elements of the design must be large. It is like furnishing a small room to make it seem larger: if we fill it up with all the usual large-room furniture in miniature size, we're conscious that everything is too small. On the contrary, if we decide on essentials and make these as large as we can—floor-to-ceiling cupboards, wall-to-wall shelves, drawers, and working tops—the proper effect is achieved. Since the outdoor scale should always stay large, if the area is small the elements must be fewer—one large tree instead of six, two or three large containers, not a dozen small ones.

This is a further reason why the usual garden-type layout is unlikely to be successful. It must necessarily be a scaled-down garden, with flowerbeds and grass areas (they cannot be called lawns) combined with paths in a fidgety jigsaw of miniature units, often fenced off from each other to make the fragmentation complete. The garden is not only the wrong character and the wrong size, it is also the wrong scale. The area would seem very much larger, as well as composing with its surroundings, if instead of the ground-level patchwork of three separate elements (paths, grass, and beds), the paving of the surrounding streets was simply continued uninterrupted through the open space and if, instead of flowers in small beds, flowers were in large containers, with a single tree growing directly from the paving.

The scale of the design would then be that of the scene it is part of: the tree large enough to register with the surrounding buildings, and the buildings reduced from a towering concrete version of a garden fence to an architectural back-cloth for branches and foliage; the flowers in their containers not miniature garden beds but large-scale pot plants for an outdoor room.

If we grow plants in large containers rather than small beds, it both transposes them to a different range of scale and puts them in a different category. They are now something added: they do not, as beds do, break up the ground surface, they are superimposed on it, and the single paved surface flows uninterrupted round and beneath them, a continuation of the general urban floor effortlessly combining this now-urban space with the city it belongs to. The plants are performers giving a self-conscious display: they are not natural, and if they seem so it is because they are accomplished

Hard and soft landscape in a small urban area. Wide steps, uninterrupted surfaces, a single tree. Large scale in a small space.

Flowers are added not in small-scale beds, but in large-scale containers on large-patterned paving (Hilles Library, Cambridge, Mass.).

actors—that is, they have been arranged by accomplished designers. The world's most accomplished IN planters are the Japanese in their small courtyard and teahouse gardens.

GRASS OR PAVING

The most effective single feature in unifying the design of any space is the treatment of the ground level, and the simplest method is to cover the ground with a uniform surface—wall-to-wall floor covering in a house, grass throughout a park or garden, and paving in urban spaces. Paving is almost always more suitable than grass, and should be considered as the standard ground cover unless there are reasons against it. Its merits are both practical and aesthetic. The practical are obvious—that it stands intensive wear, is clean and dry to walk on in all weathers, and needs little maintenance. The aesthetic merits are various and some have already been mentioned—that its character is urban, for instance, and that by continuing the ground surface of the surrounding areas the flow of space is unbroken. Paving also makes an excellent setting for vegetation, both because its simple surface is an ideal foil for

Paving in an urban garden (Piccadilly, London).

Soft bricks instead of grass as contrast with paving (Cambridge, Mass.).

Gravel is also an alternative but needs more upkeep (city centre, Hartford, Conn.).

organic forms, and more practically because it protects the roots of trees and shrubs in heavily used areas. These grow well through gaps in paving. In fact, the greatest advantage of paving over grass is that it can support a great deal of vegetation in a small space, since the ground walked on can also provide root run for large plants.

In the city landscape grass sterilises the limited areas of ground available for use or for growing plants, it provides no decoration, no composition, no third dimension. It is in effect an impractical form of hard landscape—a level ground surface which happens to be green but cannot be walked on, and though much cheaper to lay than paving, more costly to maintain.

PLANT CONTAINERS

Containers, like everything else, should be simple and large-scale whatever their shape, and like all other furniture in these outdoor rooms—litter bins, lights, signs, seats—should be of the highest possible level of design: simple, solid, and unselfconscious. They should also ideally be designed in a common idiom, so that a seat and the litter bin beside it form a harmonious group. Surely in this mass-produced age there is no difficulty (and potentially much saving) in commissioning a set of good designs and making them standard for an area.

But since Utopia has not yet arrived, and since cheap and simple plant containers are meanwhile hard to come by, why not use the large concrete rings of underground piping systems? (Or whatever it is one sees on the verges of motorways in construction.) These come in a wide range of diameters, are completely simple, and are made of the same material as the paving they will be used with (stone flags being an unlikely luxury). Also, since they are merely rings without bottoms, there is the great advantage that they can be set over gaps in the paving so that the soil they contain is continuous with the ground beneath, thus providing drainage, and—far more important—reducing the need for watering. For once established, the roots of plants reach down to the deeper moister soil. Shrubs and even trees could no doubt be grown in the larger rings, which would protect them from injury above the ground yet leave their roots unrestricted.

We know very little about growing plants in containers, however. Bottomless rings merely avoid the problem, since essen-

Street furniture designed as a whole and on an outdoor scale as companion to the architecture (Government Center, Boston, Mass.).

Concrete rings as plant containers added to an area of existing pavement. If the paving has been opened below, then the trees will root deeply and need no watering (London).

Trees in containers designed with the building, but unless the bottom is open to a deeper root-run, the trees will need constant watering and their size will be limited (New York).

tially the plants are growing directly in the ground. Certainly this is always best where possible, but often it is not, and in future cities the honest and uninterrupted earth will become a rare luxury for urban vegetation. What of open spaces with basements beneath, or the roofs of buildings? What of the multilevel cities predicted for the future? Already large underground structures like carparks isolate the shallow surface soil from the deep moist layers essential for vegetation in summer. For it is not simply the summer rainfall of temperate climates which supports temperate summer vegetation. The deep ground absorbs and holds water for long periods, making winter rain available for summer growth—a long-term storage process by which streams may run with water that fell as rain months or even years before. And the process is widespread as well as long-term, producing a general level of ground water over large areas. Unless this were so trees could not flourish unwatered in city pavements, where the ground surface for acres around is cut off from all rainfall by a waterproof lid of roads and buildings.

A private advantage of separate containers—the garden moves with the occupants.
(Though the workmen resent the fall in status of moving plants instead of furniture.)
London.

Isolated from this fundamental insurance of reliable sustenance, the life of plants in containers is a chancy business relying on human ministrations—as everyone knows who has coped with even the small-scale container plant growing of window boxes. Leave them unwatered for a hot week of summer holiday, and we come back to dead flowers as dry as last year's hay. Larger plants in larger containers will produce larger problems, and we need far more information, such as which plants do best in these unnatural conditions. Small spaces enclosed by walls may be unhealthily hot or equally unhealthily dark. What particular species of trees and shrubs and flowers best survive these trials? What types of containers are most efficient? The longest-lasting? What are the best methods of watering, feeding, and so on?

For small areas plants in containers have certain advantages, especially with new techniques of automatic watering (otherwise holiday arrangements are as necessary as for pets). But even if in larger areas larger containers hold shrubs and small trees, in the context of huge modern buildings they are reduced to mere outdoor pot plants, and for vegetation large enough to register in multilevel cities we shall need to train up tall trees in spaces between the buildings, with their crowns branching out at the higher levels. This is already being done at motorway crossings, where trees planted at the ground level of the lower road rise leafily to flyover level, combining (if not exactly reconciling) the road with the area it bestrides.

HARD SURFACES

Hard landscaping is generally thought of as inorganic, as the inert and probably synthetic element of the scene in contrast to the natural living vegetation. But this is only partly true, and in the close-up conditions of small urban spaces the hard surfaces can themselves have organic character. Stone paving in old towns, for instance, worn and weathered to the natural grain, is as intimately part of the organic world as the bark of a tree or the rocks of a seashore. The texture of granite setts, the rounded shapes of water-worn cobbles—these are organic elements in the landscape, even if not living. Water always and everywhere is actively alive, and in the urban scene so are the shadows of vegetation. Clearly defined shadows are a pleasure specific to the built environment, since it is only man-made surfaces which provide the smooth

planes where shadows show in detailed outline. And the shadows
of leaves on walls and pavements are a particular delight of the
urban scene, an organic pattern of shifting dapples of light and dark,
merging in ever-changing permutations of soft-edged shapes.

TREES IN CITIES

But though shadows may change dead concrete to an organic surface, the shadows depend on trees overhead, and trees are
the vegetation *par excellence* for cities for two main reasons. First,
as elsewhere, because they are large enough to register on the large
scale, and particularly because they have vertical mass—they are
tall enough to compose with the tall buildings of the central urban
setting. That this large mass—and a fully grown tree is an enormous
structure—can find space in the dense fabric of city centres is due
to a second advantage: their piloti structure.

The ground level of cities is intensively used. There could
never be any question of occupying the space with the mass of a

A landscape of built structures and IN *planting—the enclosed spaces roofed
and furnished with trees as a decorative overhead canopy on clear-pruned trunks.
A progression through Harvard Yard (Cambridge, Mass.) . . .*

tree at the crowded circulation level of people and traffic. The shrub and herb layer in fact is already fully occupied by human beings—it is a further reason why the ordinary garden layout is fundamentally unsuitable: it competes with us and our traffic. Only high-level space is readily available for city vegetation, and only trees with their conveniently small trunks can occupy this overhead region without also occupying the ground level.

Structure suits trees to high-density areas in a further way. The leafy parts of plants are as vulnerable to destruction by careless humans in cities as to being eaten by hungry animals in the wild—low-level vegetation is always at the mercy of low-level creatures. In a city, shrubs and flowers can survive only in beds or containers, grass only with the protection of railings or PLEASE KEEP OFF notices. But trees carry their vulnerable leaves high above harm's way, on solid trunks protected by woody bark. They are as safe from harm in a crowded city as in a sheltered garden, and with their roots protected by paving are undisturbed by the daily thousands who may pass beneath them.

A clear paved ground surface also makes easy the clearing up of the inevitable litter of much-used areas—by no means simple

Trees carefully preserved in the narrow strip between new buildings and the new road-widening. Their piloti structure makes vegetation possible in this busy main road with no available ground space (Marylebone Road, London).

with beds of flowers and entangling shrubs. A composition of ground-level vegetation is all too easily infected by the imperfections of the ground-level scene, not only litter but all the general accretions of the city floor. Trees exist serene and immaculate in the empty air above our earthbound mess. We can admire their beauties with sky for background.

EFFECTS OF TREES ON SCALE

Another, and entirely unexpected, virtue of trees in a restricted space is that they make the space appear larger. This unlikely result seems completely illogical, since we should expect that adding extra mass to a limited space would make it feel congested and therefore smaller. But on the contrary trees seem to expand the space and push back its boundaries. The enclosing walls seem farther away.

There are various reasons for this effect. One is that because the surrounding walls are partly hidden we are less conscious of being enclosed. We may even unconsciously discount the hidden

Trees enlarge this narrow space—

And transform this narrow defile.

boundaries and feel that the space we are in extends indefinitely beyond the screen—as a curtain on the wall of a room creates the illusion of space beyond. Another reason is that the scale of trees at close quarters (bark and leaves and twigs) is small compared with that of the surrounding buildings, and this general scaling down of our standard of judgement has the effect of enlarging the space. It is the same effect which makes a furnished room seem larger than the same room unfurnished: there is less actual space, but since we judge by a different scale the room as a whole seems larger.

Related to this, and probably the most important reason, is that the trees create a more completely enclosed space and therefore change our entire experience of the space as environment. That the outdoor scale is much larger than the indoor is a well-known fact, but it nonetheless never ceases to surprise us in application. The rooms of a half-built house, for instance, which seem when open foundations to be minute enclosures habitable only by dwarfs, change size completely as soon as the walls are up and the roof on. We now judge the enclosed space by the small scale of the indoor environment and the rooms become vastly larger. In the same way trees, by roofing and furnishing a space, can translate it to an outdoor room and thus enlarge it in our consciousness. Therefore, planting trees in small spaces can make them seem larger and less restricting. A single tree can transform a cramped space between buildings from a narrow well to a sheltered courtyard.

TREES NEAR BUILDINGS

Trees near buildings are by no means the obvious danger they are often made out to be—certainly not to buildings with modern foundations. Underground services are a greater difficulty, but by far the biggest problem is not underground but above. It is the problem of cutting out light. Trees near buildings are far more likely to cause trouble by shading the windows than by disturbing the walls the windows are built in. For trees that are worth having grow large and can rob us of the sun we all want in our rooms (all, that is, who do not work in modern glass towers), and it is therefore essential, if trees are not to be horribly mutilated as they grow large, to choose their position with an exact idea of their shade when fully grown. Which way is the sun? Will the tree shade windows? Are they the windows of rooms people use? *When* do they use them? (Evening and early morning sun is irrelevant to working hours and office windows.) Will the shade be in high-sun, short-shadow summer, or only in low-sun winter when the branches are bare?

LIGHT AND SHADE

Often problems of shaded windows can be avoided simply by siting a tree at one side rather than another of a given space, or sometimes by planting at the edge of the area so that its shadow falls on the road, not the buildings. There is also the new situation of wanting not summer *sun* but summer *shade* in the greenhouse rooms behind the glass walling of many new city buildings.

In America, with a more extreme climate, shade is valued more than in Britain, and it is much more common to see large deciduous species growing close to buildings. Generally, tall species

Two ailanthus trees growing from the very foundations of a house which seems none the worse. Shaping to let in the light by lower branches carefully taken off flush with the trunk (London).

Even with new buildings some people have faith in their foundations. The birch used for the filigree pattern outlined against the wall (St. Paul's Choir School).

A weeping ash, not a willow but equally overwhelming. In the local gardens competition, the long-suffering owners were given a special prize for living in private gloom for the sake of public green.

with high overhead canopies (the American elm was the ideal tree before it was struck by the Dutch elm disease) should be planted on the south side, while windows on the west should be shaded with lower-growing species to give shade against the sinking afternoon sun, the most troublesome.

A tree may sometimes mean sun, not shade. In a sunless space between high buildings, a tree may catch the light because it rises above the buildings' shadows, and by thus making the sunlight visible can bring the effect of sun into gloomy spaces.

The shade of trees in the open is a separate consideration, but shade is in any case relative. The adjustment of the eye-brain system to light is astonishingly efficient. The difference in intensity between twilight and bright sunlight may be as much as a thousand times, yet we can see to read in both. Admittedly we accommodate to this vast range gradually, but when we walk in or out of a house,

A tree brings light into a shady square.

The cheerful shade of deciduous trees.

the light intensity changes by as much as a factor of ten; yet this seldom troubles us—mostly we are scarcely conscious of the change. The shade of trees out-of-doors is therefore not important for vision. The decrease in light value is slight compared with the difference between indoors and out, and our eyes adjust automatically. What matters is the emotional effect of the shade—does it strike us as gloomy and therefore depressing? Or is it pleasant, like the shade of a tree-lined road?

Actually the shade of deciduous trees is seldom gloomy, for since their leaves are translucent the light is not blocked but filtered by growth patterns of the foliage. Species of trees for built-up areas where light may be a problem should be chosen to cast a light shade—tall and sparsely branching and without heavy foliage. It may also be necessary to thin the crown of trees so as to remove some of their mass and let in more light. This is one of the legitimate reasons for pruning, but the thinning must be done with understanding care and in sympathy with the tree's natural structure, so that it produces not a differently shaped tree but only a less solid tree. Generally whole boughs should be taken out low down and flush with the trunk, so that the upward growth of the tree flows past to the branches above. Otherwise a thicket of new shoots will break out from every amputation, destroying the tree's shape and making it far thicker than before.

The effect we want beneath trees in towns is not solid shade but textured light, an atmospheric pattern of shadows and half-shadows, of filtered shine and bright shafts of sun. In spring, when the young leaves are thin and pale, light through the filmy yellow green creates an effect of sunlight even in grey weather.

THE STRUCTURE OF TREES

Trees which in the open landscape appear thin and open are often ideally suited to urban conditions. Conversely, trees which are used in OUT planting to create solid mass (such as the horse chestnut) are usually too dense for IN planting. The intimate structure of twigs and branches is significant here too, since far more than in the open we are conscious of their pattern in space—not simply the outline space in which a tree or shrub exists, but also the volume of space contained within the scaffolding of branches.

"Take a single tree only," said Uvedale Price, "and consider it in this point of view [the quality of "intricacy"]. It is composed of millions of boughs, sprays, and leaves, intermixed with and crossing each other in as many directions; while through the various openings, the eye still discovers new and infinite combinations of them: yet in this labyrinth of intricacy, there is no unpleasant confusion; the general effect is as simple as the detail is complicated."

In trees which we live close to in the built environment this interior structure is very important. When we fell a tree, said Thoreau, we "lay waste the air." For a tree is far more than its own material mass: it is also the volume of air it occupies, the pattern it makes of the space it appropriates. If the mere material of a tree were compacted to a solid, like an automobile in a car-crushing plant, then (also like the car) it would take up only a very small part of the volume of space it actually occupies—what we think of as the automobile or the tree. Within its outline shape most of a tree is interior space, and this is distinctively organised by the habit of growth of the particular tree and the particular species.

Depending roughly on the solidity of the tree's mass there are three general types of organisation—patterned, structured, and occupied space. Patterned space is created by sparsely growing trees and shrubs. We are conscious of the tree less as a mass than as a volume of space which it has appropriated and made part of its structure, and within this volume the material of the tree creates a three-dimensional filigree pattern of branches and leaves. This is a common growth pattern in desert climates but not in the temperate, though the indigenous birch is a filigree tree, and so is the acacia, introduced from drier climates.

In the second type, structured space, the growth pattern of the tree moulds and defines the volume of space contained within it. It creates not an overall mesh pattern but a complex composition of masses and voids. Cedars are an obvious example of structured space, and such trees as maples grow in less clearly defined planes.

Occupied space is simple: it is the volume occupied by the mass of a tree as a whole. The tree seems solid with no internal space, only an outline mass in the general space of the environment. Horse chestnuts in particular grow to this solid mass, as do such conifers as cypresses and many shrubs. These are the trees which in landscape design are nearest to the masses of architecture, and they are best used as mass in the open landscape. In the built-up environment they tend to be too overpoweringly solid; they are also dull, since they screen all views of the tree's internal structure and its patterns of light and shade.

Gilpin had no doubt about it: "An over-loaded foliage destroys all form. The point of picturesque perfection is when the tree has foliage enough to form a mass, and yet not so much as to hide the branches. One of the great ornaments of a tree is its ramification, which ought to appear, here and there, under the foliage, even when it is in full leaf." (He would approve of the Berkeley Square pruning, see p. 212.)

The essentially different growth patterns of trees mean that if any pruning or cutting out of branches is necessary (as it may be to keep space open or to let in light), it should be done with great care to preserve the tree's health and equally its inherent structure. Every tree—certainly every species of tree—needs pruning to a specific framework to suit its individual vegetable architecture.

FOLIAGE IN TOWNS

If, in IN planting, habit is the most important quality of vegetation, then the next is foliage—as everyone knows who grows house plants—and though foliage too is always important, it has different values in IN and OUT planting. In the open it provides texture and superimposed pattern in a general green background, but in an enclosed space leaves take on a distinct identity of their own. Outlined against a building, the shape of a leaf is as significant as the shape of a flower. Large leaves of bold and distinctive shape have a sculptural quality; pinnate leaves produce intricate double patterns of leaves and leaflets; elegantly outlined leaves are seen to perfection.

For similar reasons the value of colour is different in the two kinds of planting, since the open scene is predominantly green and contrast will therefore depend on flowers or on the variations in the colour of foliage—paler or darker green, golden, copper, glaucous, and so on—or more subtly on differences of texture and reflection of light. Without this variety the open scene is monotonous and lacks interest, but this is not so with IN planting. Here buildings provide the contrast and variety of colour. Since the background is not green but usually a neutral buffish grey, green now becomes a vivid and distinctive colour in its own right with no need of variation. Foliage which in the open scene may be acceptable as a contrast, such as golden privet (a much-maligned and cruelly overclipped shrub), will, as IN planting, provide less contrast against light-coloured walls than ordinary darker shrubs, and certainly be less satisfactory than natural leaf-green. Colour, in fact, except organic green, is not primarily what we need from IN planting. Colour is far simpler to provide on walls than in vegetation. If we want yellow, for instance, why not paint a yellow panel behind a green plant? It is far more effective than yellow foliage against a neutral wall, even more than a fleeting display of yellow flowers.

Another quality of vegetation which we seldom consciously notice is its movement. In the open landscape trees sway in the wind, shrubs toss, leaves flutter, grass flows like water—the organic scene naturally responds to wind and weather. But not the built landscape. It is part of the strangeness of a city to a country person that a wind which would set the whole countryside in motion has no effect on the rigid surfaces of walls and paved earth, and that unless the view from our window includes vegetation (or flying

In our new glass and concrete cities, reflections add life to inert structures.

The ambiguous townscape of mirror walls.

litter) we have no way of telling whether the outside air is a dead calm or blowing a gale.

Against rigid surfaces, therefore, the movement of plants and the varying patterns of their movement have a new intensity. The fluttering of poplars and birches, the streaming motion of lanceolate leaves, plane leaves which pan horizontally on their long stalks, the peculiar sideways movement of single ash leaves in a light breeze, the pliancy of bare birch twigs and branches which sway like a blown fountain in winter winds—movements which we only vaguely notice in the open—become vivid and intimate pleasures in an urban space, and plants can be used as superb organic mobiles in a built-up urban scene.

Shadows too are a decorative element of IN planting as they never can be in the open landscape. There the surfaces are too broken to show more than a general shade, and even closely mown grass shows little detail. But the exactly outlined shadows on urban surfaces should always be remembered in planting design.

Above all, any plant chosen for an urban setting must be

Shadows make organic patterns on a new-world wall (Euston Station, London).

attractive all year round. For as a camera picks out a particular figure in a crowd and examines it in close-up, so IN planting picks out particular plants from the general vegetation and examines them in intimate isolation. Flowers are easily provided by bulbs and summer planting; permanent vegetation must be chosen for its year-round qualities. Good habit, good foliage, good winter effect—these matter infinitely more than flowers in urban plants, which must be chosen not as casual acquaintances we meet now and then, but as close companions we live with all the time.

7.
Landscape maintenance

A man-made landscape depends on two things: first, the original design; second, the subsequent maintenance. These are of equal importance, for since the material of landscape is in a constant state of change, the way these changes are managed will affect the design profoundly, and if handled badly may even lead to its destruction. The vicissitudes of the French royal park at Versailles show this very clearly. Laid out by Le Nôtre in a strictly formal style, the vegetation was disciplined to an absolute perfection of green architecture—not a leaf out of place. This superb intellectual composition was royally maintained through the eighteenth century up to the French Revolution, when the aristocracy and most of the aristocratic parks were swept away together.

Versailles, however, was not destroyed; it was merely neglected. The tyrannised vegetation, like the tyrannised population, was freed by revolution, and grew away unhindered in its own natural growth patterns. The formal parterres became tangled meadows, the clipped hedges spread to bushy thickets, plashed trees grew free to woodland glades. Without maintenance, the intellectually disciplined formal landscape disappeared and the classical park became a romantic wilderness.

Maintenance, then, is essential. It is also expensive and increasingly hard to come by. Where there were ten men in the past there is now only one, and what of the future as wages continue to rise? Maintenance is already a major problem, and most areas will have to survive with minimum care. In any landscape the maintenance likely to be available, in terms of both cost and skills, must be a decisive factor in the design, and to lay out an area without knowing whether anyone will maintain it, or without leaving any instructions as to the methods to be used, is as unrealistic as to take a house without knowing whether we can pay the rent. It is not only new landscapes that we need. We must also have methods of maintenance that suit the way these landscapes will be used as well as the way they are planted.

No good ignoring awkward maintenance (even though there seems no great demand for this particular drowned seat).

WOODLAND MANAGEMENT

If natural mixed woodland is left to itself with no maintenance of any kind it will clearly survive. But compared with woodland sympathetically managed, it will not be particularly attractive to human beings. There will be trees in all stages of life and death and trouble with pests, a woodland floor cluttered with decaying vegetation, and probably impenetrable thickets of understory shrubs. Nor is such woodland easily usable for recreation or anything else, and some kind of maintenance is needed to adapt it to use.

But what maintenance and what use? There are already various established systems of managing forest for timber, and the woodlands of commercial forestry can, with relatively minor adaptations, be used for recreation of various kinds, as they are already in both Britain and America. But most woodlands in the areas where we live are not commercial forests, and their management will depend on their other uses. London's Epping Forest, for in-

The notice is about what one may or may not do on this vanished open space (Surrey).

stance, is managed for recreation. There are paths through the trees, open glades and vistas, a clear forest floor for walking, areas for parking cars and picnicking, and a varied pattern of open grassy spaces, shrubby thickets, and woodland dense enough for the shy wild deer to survive despite thousands of visitors to what is a comparatively small area.

In America, the management of woodland for uses other than timber is not a question of a few hundred acres but of millions. In Connecticut alone there are 2 million acres of forest (almost as

Footpath in Epping Forest.

A woodland area arranged for car-parking with footpaths and picnic areas (Ashridge, Hertfordshire).

much as the woodlands of the whole of England), and the Agricultural Experimental Station founded in 1875 for the benefit of farming is now concerned with the management of the suburban forest that has replaced the farmland. Managing how and for what? The Lockwood Conference in 1962 began by defining its subject: "The suburban forest is that part of our forest land which is man-oriented. It is the land surrounding and permeating the clearings for cities, farms, homes, and highways. This land contains sufficient trees to give a wooded appearance . . . provides privacy, varied scenery, recreation, and a backdrop against which man carries out his daily activities." The suburban forest, then, is an amenity forest; it must be fairly stable and trouble-free, giving privacy but not obstruction; it must be diverse enough to provide a home for desirable wildlife but must be free from other wildlife (rats, mosquitoes, and so on).

The methods suggested at the Lockwood Conference for producing such woodland were various, and, as we should expect in a forest climate, were chiefly concerned with creating or maintaining open space—cutting and grazing, preventing new growth by herbicide sprays, removing organic matter from the forest to discourage vigorous growth, selective felling and clearing of different areas in rotation so that some open space would always be present, as well as all stages of the succession. This last is a process which in a specialised version already exists in England's New Forest. Where use is intensive such maintenance may also need to include positive measures, such as arranging for regeneration or replanting, protecting the forest floor from too much trampling, and so on.

ESTABLISHING NEW WOODLAND

The maintenance needed for newly planted or regenerating amenity woodland is another matter. In nature most trees grow up in the shelter of either other trees or shrubs: they do not compete directly with herbs like long grass or bracken; or if they do it is commonly in conditions of semishade to which young trees are better adapted than their rivals. When trees once grow clear of the herb layer—certainly above the shrub layer—they are more or less safe, and their subsequent growth will control other vegetation and create the conditions that suit themselves.

If planted directly in grass, young trees are at risk for the first few years, either from competition for water and nutrients by the weeds or simply from being smothered by the grass. The fire hazard in suburban areas is also very serious at this critical stage. A very little help can make all the difference between death and survival. Keeping down (not removing, merely discouraging) grass and weeds immediately around the new trees for the first few years is generally enough to ensure that they grow on with little further maintenance. It is like balancing a see-saw when a very slight push will bring it down on the side we want.

OPEN-SPACE MANAGEMENT

We do not always want woodland, no matter how attractive it is, and the usual function of maintenance is to establish and preserve a landscape composed of a mosaic of different layers— trees, shrubs, herbaceous plants, and a mosslike layer of mown grass. Maintenance is thus a composite business and, as stated earlier,

An eighteenth-century landscape park of masses and spaces where golf is maintaining the open space. (Nothing is maintaining the open lake.) Leeds Castle, Kent.

except for the fully developed tree layer, consists of checking or arresting the natural progression of the vegetation towards forest and of holding the different types of plants at that stage of their development which suits our design. In fact, in most of our landscape maintenance is the maintenance of space. In a temperate forest habitat it is not mass but space which is the difficult element to preserve. Without maintenance, space is lost by the overgrowth of mass, and the more complex the space the more maintenance is needed to preserve it. Bare ground needs more labour than grass, mown grass than rough grass, grass than shrubs, shrubs than trees. And low-level space takes more effort to preserve than high-level space, since more layers of the vegetation are omitted.

The task of maintaining spaces is a factor to consider in the design layout. Most maintenance will be by machines which are only awkwardly manoeuverable, and to be worked efficiently, the areas where they operate must be planned in terms of their movement.

DESIGN, STYLE, AND MAINTENANCE COSTS

The landscape style as well as the landscape layout depends on maintenance. Obviously the less maintenance available, the less we can depart from the natural growth processes of vegetation. The

High-grade maintenance in a seventeenth-century formal garden (Kew)—

formal style can never be low-maintenance, since it uses vegetation in ways completely alien to its natural growth and is achieved only by coercion. If plants are to be used as architecture the design must be as plant, not human, architecture to survive without constant reinforcement. In eighteenth-century parks plants were used as vegetable compositions with their own inherent structure. The trees were free-growing; the art was in the grouping, the proportions, the omissions. The low-maintenance cost of landscape parks compared with that of the formal gardens they replaced was thoroughly appreciated by their eighteenth-century owners. Even in those days of cheap and plentiful labour, low maintenance was a cogent reason for their sweeping popularity.

"I will be bold to affirm," said Stephen Switzer, "that £10 will go as far in this rural Gardening as £50 will in the methods commonly taken. Being of a much more natural aspect than Set Gardening the less keeping will suffice."

No formal styles, then, for low-cost maintenance, and also very few flowerbeds. Flowers are a luxury. They need too much care to use in any but high-maintenance areas; on a limited income they are a lavish extravagance which we should indulge in only

And an informal city centre (Hartford, Conn.). Un air paré *is essential here.*

for chosen situations where they will give proportionate pleasure. For there is no such thing as a labour-saving flowerbed or an easy herbaceous border. Those who believe so are millionaires economising on their second chauffeur. Certainly there are a few vigorous perennials which will more or less hold their own in chosen corners without help, but flowers in weeded beds are pampered beauties, and we should associate with them warily. "These are easy flowers," so the gardening books assure us; "they need no more than routine weeding and a yearly top dressing." "Easy"; "no more than"—but top dressing every year and weeding beds all through the growing season are a princely service. If such "easy" plants were left alone to compete with the natives, they would quickly disappear without trace.

Another inescapable fact is that the less money and skills available for future maintenance the more care is needed for the initial design. If unlimited maintenance can be taken for granted then there is nothing simpler than to lay out an attractive arrangement of lawns and flowerbeds and flowering shrubs. This happens far too often, and the result is that either design or finances must suffer—either there is an increased burden of cost for upkeep, or

Drawing-board layout for maximum maintenance—the grass strips too narrow for easy mowing, the curb not used to contain the grass but cut away to double the edging; the flowers tender bedding species which constantly need renewing.

In any case, both the high-grade maintenance and the two-dimensional pattern of beds in grass are unsuitable in this harsh and large-scale setting. Here nothing would register but a clump of large trees—and there's plenty of room for them.

else a scene whose attraction depends on high maintenance becomes ill-kept and slatternly.

Less future maintenance, therefore, means more present care: it also means extra cost in the original laying out. Grass, for instance, is commonly the cheapest way of surfacing an area—in most temperate climates it will more or less establish itself—but over the years of routine cutting, mown grass makes one of the most expensive landscapes to maintain. (In the same way, cotton shirts may be cheaper to buy than drip-dry fabrics—but who pays for the ironing?)

To cut down the original once-only cost at the expense of the perpetually recurring cost of upkeep is clearly an irresponsible extravagance. For the cost of a design is not simply the price of its layout—though often this alone is estimated. The true cost is the price of the layout plus the annual maintenance (say, even for a ten-year period), and if assessed by this obviously realistic method, many cut-price designs would be revealed as prodigally expensive. A comparison of figures will show that formal bedding-out is the most expensive, with costs decreasing thereafter for mixed shrub

Even with this formal garden style a different layout could halve the maintenance —mown lawns, clipped edges, dead-headed roses, raked-in-petals, trimmed hedges, and the bank mown by strong young men pulling a mower up and down by hand (Regent's Park).

and herbaceous areas, mown grass (cut fourteen or fifteen times a year), cut grass (cut three or four times a year), and finally, the least costly, trees.

HIGH-MAINTENANCE LANDSCAPES

The expense of high-maintenance landscapes is not the only objection to them; their style is equally undesirable in many situations where grounds need looking after. The land uses of our new industrial society produce a great many areas where the landscape must be managed and kept tidy by specific action but where a high-grade maintenance style is completely out of place. Informal recreation areas are an obvious example. Close-mown lawns and tended beds are no setting for kickabouts, dog-chasing, and general exuberant running around. These need a robust and simple landscape of rough-cut grass, indestructible shrubs, and free-growing damage-proof trees.

Nor does an indiscriminate high-maintenance landscape make an attractive setting for the medium-density living areas of many suburbs. Detached or semidetached houses on small plots of land are common in Britain and increasingly so in America, and generally the surroundings, both private and public, are depressingly overmaintained. Few landscapes are more boring than those where the natural growth of vegetation is everywhere cut back, not for any reasons of design, only from a passion for tidiness or love of domination.

In gardens high maintenance should be concentrated on encouraging treasured plants to grow more freely: the arrangement is for the benefit of the chosen vegetation. True gardeners love plants, but maintenance lovers do not. They see all spontaneous growth as a challenge to their authority—if not as actual criminal revolution.

So skimpy planting, grass and shrubs pared back to the quick, trees spaced out in solitary confinement—such starveling landscapes are depressingly common everywhere, and doubly depressing because their creators clearly must mean well. But this is not vegetation as the green environment; it is vegetation as material for exercising machines. There is no sense of the organic life of growing things that is so refreshingly different from our man-made world of bricks and concrete.

"Dressed ground," says Thomas Whately, "has such an

Differently maintained neighbors—

In the same country lane. But in private landscape whichever we like best is best.

appearance of having been made by a receipt, that curiosity, that most active principle of pleasure, is almost extinguished. Monotony and baldness are the great defects of improved places."

"NATURAL" LANDSCAPES

So why "improve" our landscapes at all if the results are so often unfortunate? "I have seen [so] many Gardens that a green Meadow is a more delightful object," complained John Rea three centuries ago, and he would see many more today. Since we all love the country, and since nothing could be more delightful than flowery meadows flowing up to our doorstep, why bother with any other landscape? Why not simply leave the countryside as we find it, as a charming rural setting for our urbanised lives?

If we propose this seriously it only shows how thoroughly we are out of touch with country realities, how incorrigibly urban. For meadows do not exist because we like the look of them on our doorstep; they exist because they are cropped and cared for by hard-working farmers making a living. Remove the farmers and

The woodland floor is as vulnerable as a flowerbed, and this carpet of bluebells will soon disappear when the wood is used by people from a new housing area planned nearby (New Ash Green).

we remove their countryside with them, and even if we could preserve the country landscape by some form of nonfarming maintenance, it is too vulnerable a landscape to live in. The country survives only in country conditions, and these do not include large numbers of free-ranging human beings. A mown lawn lives through walking on because it is maintained as a walking surface; a meadow does not because it is grown as a crop. In the United States the natural woodland does not survive intensive use. Existing trees are more or less safe, but the seedlings and ground-level flowers are quickly lost. The forest becomes no longer naturally self-perpetuating.

Nonetheless architects (beginning with Corbusier) draw entrancing sketches of apartment complexes in undisturbed flowery grass. If the meadows survive the flat builders (unlikely), they would certainly not survive the flat inhabitants. Roses round the door flourish because they are recognised as unnatural and carefully cherished: wild flowers round the same door are considered as natural and expected to survive by themselves, with the result that they quickly perish.

The natural habitat modified for use. Local heather instead of grass, with local rocks and a group of local birches. Surfaced path to take the wear. An interesting experiment, but grass is invading heather in the changed conditions (Cumbernauld).

Rosa vincit omnia. *Roses planted as hopeful transformation of derelict land around storage sheds. Nature is doing a much better landscape job in the background with hundreds of self-sown birches.*

GARDEN-STYLE LANDSCAPES

High-cost, high-labour maintenance is equally unsuitable for the increasingly large areas of land which now need managing around institutions, factories, service structures like roads and power stations, and all the rest. A garden style is here completely incongruous, yet we see large buildings (concerned with either a better image or a better environment) set in a pathetic patch of shaved grass and bedded-out flowers, even though the landscape as a whole is neglected and near-derelict. The maintenance expended on mowing and weeding this skimped nongarden would, if differently used, be enough to manage the whole area as a suitable setting for the structures within it. Such a scene needs *vegetation,* not *control* of vegetation—plenty of free-growing large-scale green as frame and screen and coordination—managed by a simple system aimed to keep the masses roughly as intended and the open spaces usable.

Road verges, too, especially along main roads and near towns, are commonly maintained with a far higher than necessary

Compromise on an American parkway. Garden maintenance backed by wild, but less lawn would make the effect less suburban.

level of mown grass and garden-style shrubs. If left to grow more freely, the verges would be far more attractive, even near cities, and maintenance costs would certainly be less than with present parkway style.

At present, in fact, there is no recognised standard: maintenance means garden maintenance and is the only system commonly practised. This is understandable if we realize how recent a development are the kinds of land use which need a different style. Recreation areas, suburbs, the grounds of industrial structures—these are new kinds of landscape that have not yet developed an appropriate *style,* much less an appropriate or understood system of maintenance.

In the agricultural past, man-made scenery was either urban, or rural countryside managed by farming. City-fringe and suburban landscapes barely existed. The only land which needed maintenance as such was gardens, and a system of weeding and mowing and pruning developed to suit them. However, that does not suit the new-style landscapes we need for our new-style land uses. What we need now are maintenance systems ranging from

The choppers and loppers had a field day—literally. These trees are on a common away from any buildings.

Different maintenance for different uses. The change from high-grade to wild marks the change from walking area to cliff edge.

high-grade to minimal, methods clearly worked out and as commonly understood as the present ubiquitous weed-and-mow, and governed by appropriateness, available labour, and intended use.

Different maintenance for different areas. The free-growing vegetation of a woodland garden becomes mown lawn and formal shrubs round the house.

INTENSIVE MAINTENANCE

High-grade maintenance should be an unmistakable category, in definite contrast to other landscape. It is not natural and need not appear so. "Apparent art," said Shenstone, "in its proper province is almost as important as apparent nature. They contrast agreeably; but their province ever should be kept distinct."

This apparent art is the particular charm of high-grade maintenance. Well-groomed, well-mannered, disciplined, elegant, sophisticated—high-grade maintenance should be all these things. This is where the formal style belongs, with its carpet lawns, architectural hedges, symmetrical flowerbeds, and trees ranged in avenues. Such a style must be perfectly maintained, or it fails in its effect. Even as simple a composition as a gravel walk along an avenue of trees in close-mown grass depends for its effect on a perfect gravel surface, immaculately kept grass, and trees trained to make an avenue of equal growth without gaps. In so formal an arrangement a missing tree is like a missing tooth, and if maintenance is inadequate to keep a formal layout in perfection, then better to adapt it to a less rigid style where irregularities seem a natural part of the design. High-maintenance landscape need not be formal, any more than urban styles of dressing or furnishing or other design. Modern urban styles are deliberately casual—but casual, not careless (carelessness is not a style but a negation of style). The actual operations of high-grade maintenance are perfectly well understood from centuries of gardening—weeding, mowing, edging, watering, clipping, pruning—nothing has changed except the newly mechanised tools for performing these operations. The old methods are still what we need; we are only newly efficient in applying them.

INTERMEDIATE MAINTENANCE

In the next category of maintenance, this is not so. For the intermediate style we need new systems of operation, or at least

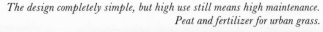

The design completely simple, but high use still means high maintenance.
Peat and fertilizer for urban grass.

Even high maintenance can't preserve grass beyond a certain level of use. A summer of visitors added to Londoners is too much for Saint James's Park. Discreet hard surfacing needed.

High-grade maintenance neglected—and no wonder. Quite apart from the flowerbeds, how does anyone mow round the railing struts? This much-used shortcut in a busy city is in any case no place for a garden which needs railings to survive (London).

the same operations differently applied for different effects. Certainly the intermediate category is not merely high-grade maintenance neglected, any more than a cherished beard is merely an unshaved stubble chin. Rough grass should be intended, not be overgrown lawn; a deliberate smother of climbers not be simply neglected; a tangle of shrubs be contained in their allotted space.

A man-made landscape must always be to some extent controlled, but the control need not be the absolute discipline we so readily impose. Barbers cut hair, but they do not crop all heads down to bristle, or short-back-and-sides, so why all grass? Hairdressers control hair, but they do not plaster it all down flat or arrange it in rows of rigid waves. Barbers and hairdressers use their maintenance methods to produce a variety of informal styles, and in landscape we could use maintenance to do the same. We should aim at the effect Horace Walpole admired in the designs of William Kent: "The living landscape was chastened and polished, not transformed."

Intermediate landscape maintenance will be transitional between high-grade and wild. It should be a flexible system deriving from both, nearer to one or the other to suit the particular situation. The control should be adequate but unobtrusive—grass cut and raked up two or three times a season (no close mowing), the layers of the vegetation casually defined, shrubs controlled by selective pruning, although no close trimming, and weeds ignored unless particularly aggressive. Most of the plants in such a landscape will be fairly tolerant of annual weed growth, and the occasional removal of weeds where they are clearly competing to the detriment of the plants is all that is necessary. In fact, some weeds can be deliberately used as ground cover to prevent other and less manageable growth. Ground elder, for instance, is excellent for underplanting around trees and shrubs. Its coarse, shallow root system is less destructive to the feeding roots of trees and shrubs than is the solidly fibrous root system of rough grass, and if mown in routine grass cutting, ground elder becomes very quickly green again and is never untidy.

Grass is by no means easily managed at this intermediate stage. Certainly it should not be mown like garden lawns, but equally it should not be cut like hay and left to rot. Not only is this unsightly, but it smothers the finer grasses and encourages coarse growth and weeds, especially in wet summers when the rotting grass may lie for weeks in mouldering swaths. Yet to rake

Hawthorns from a former field hedge "chastened and polished" for a new living area (New Ash Green).

The intermediate style for village greens. High-grade maintenance would destroy the country character.

Intermediate maintenance in a village churchyard creates a casual style which can't be planned.

A forage harvester cutting and collecting grass.

up the grass after mowing means double labour. Surely some new type of machine is needed: something which cuts long grass as existing hay cutters do but which also collects the cut grass like a lawn mower. Rotary cutters now on the market are not the answer—they neither cut hay-length grass nor collect the cuttings—but why not an adaptation of the forage harvester to cut the grass and blow or carry the cuttings into a trailer behind? (The market is surely large enough to make the cost of the experiment pay.)

SEMIWILD MAINTENANCE

Most of the techniques in the intermediate grade of maintenance are based on roughly the same principles and can use some of the same machinery as more intensive maintenance. But the third category, the semiwild, uses maintenance techniques developed from forestry, farming, and other estate management rather than from gardening. At present we have little idea of how to manage natural-looking semiwild landscapes except as woodland. In the past these have been in rural areas and were the result of some kind of nonintensive farming—generally, rough grazing. But our new urban land uses need natural-seeming landscapes (for country recreation, for instance) where maintenance by farming is no longer possible, and where specific maintenance methods must therefore be used deliberately to create the same natural effects. Commons, especially in southern England, are already clear proof of the need for such a system. These were formerly controlled by the grazing of commoners' animals, but since these have now disappeared, many commons either are turning into city parks by misguided overmaintenance or are being overrun by scrub and potential woodland, and are often scarcely usable.

On a small scale this is the beginning in England of the same natural process that in eastern America has already changed vast areas of farmland to forest. In Connecticut, for instance, there is more than half an acre of woodland per person, and the woodland's chief use is amenity. In Britain, on the other hand, the approximate acre of land per person covers every kind of landscape, including the uplands (which are roughly half our land area) and also, in the lowlands, all our high-intensity farmland, which cannot be used for recreation. Our limited country amenity areas must therefore serve greater numbers than America's extensive wood-

The semiwild on Hampstead Heath.

This churchyard wall is simply neglected—and all the better for it.

lands, and many of these areas must be managed to keep them open enough to satisfy our demand for areas for picnicking, kicking a ball around, and all the other things urban dwellers do on a day out in the country.

In Britain, as already in America, some marginal farmland is beginning to go out of cultivation, because it is no longer profitable to work by the expensive new methods of intensive farming. The best way of using such areas—certainly until needed for other land uses—is for recreation. No longer part of the farming countryside, these areas can be valuable extensions of city people's environments. Our problem in Britain, unlike the east coast of America, is that most marginal agricultural areas are less accessible to the urban commuters than the intensively agricultural areas. Disused agricultural areas need managing by a system of maintenance adapted to their specific character, which in this case is seemingly natural country, in contrast to the man-made cities. Fortunately, as William Marshall observed, "Our idea of natural is not confined to neglected nature, but extends to nature touched by art and rendered intelligible to human perception." This is also a suitable style for many other areas that will increasingly need managing in the future, as, for example, open areas in America's suburban forests, and certainly Britain's country parks, which are otherwise in danger of bearing no relationship at all to the country but of being routinely managed as municipal parks without flowers.

A seminatural style would be excellent for much city-fringe landscape—cheap to manage, providing more rural scenery for city dwellers, and checking the depressing sense of ubiquitous urban sprawl, which is often due not to the relatively sparsely built structures in the area but to the way the landscape is managed (or generally mismanaged).

We still have no recognised system for managing semiwild landscape, and though some research is already in hand, far more is needed before anyone can provide appropriate answers to the question. At present we have little knowledge of how to do it except in a one-time, hit-or-miss fashion, where ad hoc but sympathetic management of a specific area has evolved its own individual style of maintenance. Such examples could be invaluable if we considered them carefully. A great deal of pragmatic knowledge could be easily and swiftly acquired simply by studying as many existing maintenance systems as possible in a wide variety of situations and use patterns. By going out looking and asking, a vast amount of information could be collected for ecologists and estate managers to interpret and adapt to produce a general interim system of maintenance. This might not be ideal, but certainly it would be a huge improvement on anything we have now, and would also provide a basis for experimental research.

Meanwhile the grass and herb layer is as usual the most urgent problem, being the fastest-growing and least stable vegetation. In semiwild areas we could start by trying a general once-yearly cutting. If it is cut only once a year, grass is commonly best controlled by cutting it a few weeks later than farmers cut their hay (which varies with the season's weather). This gives time for the early meadow flowers to blossom, for the grasses to seed, and in rural areas for ground-nesting birds to rear their young. Subsequent growth of grass is not vigorous. In areas where late-summer flowers are also important and where little trampling takes place, it might be possible to leave the grass through the summer and to work out a system of winter clearance (possibly using burning

Olmsted's Central Park today, and surely as he intended—deliciously wild, whether from design or economy. (That it is also dangerously wild is not the fault of the design.)

in some areas) to break up tussocky growth and prevent a mat from forming, as well as to keep down seedling shrubs and trees. It would be essential to take up the yearly mowings and not leave them to rot, and again a machine based on the forage harvester might provide a combined operation.

As always, however, certain areas of higher use would also need higher maintenance. This is so even in the natural landscapes of the national parks of America, where, for instance, the paths down the Grand Canyon need maintenance against erosion. Nonetheless, the overall aim should be a landscape we accept as natural, "the spontaneous arrangements of nature improved by taste," as Horace Walpole described it (though in our more work-aday age the arrangements are more likely to be adapted to use than improved by taste).

In the built environment man is all too often and all too plainly the master; our concern should be to establish a different world by use of vegetation. As a general rule, therefore, it is best to manage any landscape at the lowest grade of maintenance which will provide for the area's use. There should always be positive reasons for interfering with the natural growth of vegetation, for it is the sense of the green environment we need to maintain, not the sense of man's domination. But perhaps we make too much fuss about maintenance, for some people find no problems. They either enjoy it ("My husband likes gardening, and I like watching him"), or else, like eleven-year-old Christine, they design to elimi-nate maintenance entirely: "I would like to live in a bunglow with two gardens, one would be for keeping flowers and would look neat, the other would be for playing and would look untidy. The sitting room would have french windows which over look the tidy garden where the flowers and rose-bushes were kept. Of course there would be artificial grass in both gardens for it would take far too much bother keeping it trim. This would mean that the flowers and rose-bushes will be artificial also and maybe once a month I would spray sent on them to give them a nice fragrance."

8.
Some notes on plants

The best guide for landscape design is landscape painting—so the eighteenth-century designers considered. But the vegetation of most landscape painters is decorative rather than organic, from the stiff two-dimensional heraldic tree patterns of the primitives to the gracefully posed undefined species which frame Claude Lorrain's romantic receding vistas. Constable's trees are alive and growing, the pre-Raphaelites' exactly identifiable, Cézanne's organic structural elements in the landscape, Derain's individual personalities. Thus the painter's treatment of trees may vary with the vision he has of nature, but the designer working with living materials is more limited in what he can do. If he plants a hundred trees it is their massing and spacing which chiefly concern him, but if he is thinking in single units then the character of the tree itself is the most important. In the eighteenth century William Marshall listed the qualities of particular concern to him: "The colour of their leaves in summer or autumn, and of their bark in winter; their times of foliation and disleafing; their manner of shooting, the structure and density of their heads, the outlines they usually take, and the heights to which they aspire—these are the properties most worthy of the attention of the artist."

For trees this does excellently as a start, though since Marshall was considering rural planting, we now need to add other qualities about trees for our modern urban and suburban landscapes. And we must also think about shrubs and flowers, while eighteenth-century designers worked only with vegetation on a grand scale.

SOME PLANTS FOR A TEMPERATE CLIMATE

Lists of plants must always be local, since with any considerable change of conditions the species that will flourish will be different. "The first thing a Gentleman does is to consider the Nature of his Soil," not only soil but temperature, rainfall, wind, exposure—the climate. There may also be considerable differences in the local soil and microclimate. Nonetheless the qualities we need in plants for design in temperate climates are similar, and we are likely to find the same qualities in similar plants for different regions.

To discuss the whole range of plants available would clearly be impossible here (because of limited knowledge as well as limited space), and in any case a large range of excellent books at every level from amateur gardening to scholarly dissertations already exists. The practical information we need for growing them is also easily available, so this chapter is limited to comments on some plants which from personal experience or observation seem particularly useful for landscape planting.*

NATIVE TREES

The ideal plants for landscape design are clearly those of the native vegetation, and the great designers used native plants almost exclusively. We begin, therefore, with trees native to a temperate climate. The traditional English oak (*Quercus robur*) is a very decorative tree, with its picturesque branching, angled pattern of twigs in winter, and interesting leaf shape. It casts a light shade, so that people as well as plants are happy beneath it, and oak woods are the richest of all in associated species of life (including insects). In poorer conditions of soil or climate the common oak is replaced by the sessile oak (*Quercus sessiliflora*). Its habit depends very much on the habitat in which it is growing. The oak in one or another species is by far the commonest tree of our natural habitats; it suits most soils, is proverbially long-lived, and if planted in close groups will grow much faster than is generally supposed. It can be used with fast-growing short-lived trees and shrubs, which will draw it up to a clear trunk before it branches, and which will die off as the developing oaks take over. The turkey oak (*Quercus cerris*), an introduced tree now naturalised in some areas, is faster-growing and less spreading, but we should use our native oaks far more than

---

Although what follows in this chapter was drawn mainly from Nan Fairbrother's English experience, most of these plants have the same names and growing habits in America. If catalogues, a local nurseryman, or a botanical garden cannot give equivalents or information about similar plants, consult The Brooklyn Botanical Garden's booklet 1200 Trees and Shrubs—Where to Buy, *which should answer most questions. The pamphlet costs $1.50 and can be obtained by writing the Garden at 1000 Washington Avenue, Brooklyn, N.Y. 11225.*

we do in landscape, both in open planting and in living areas. For despite its associations of primeval forest, the oak is not a tree of overwhelmingly forest character, as is, for instance, the beech (*Fagus sylvatica*), a native which regenerates naturally on the southern chalk and grows readily when planted in most parts of Britain (it is the commonest hedgerow tree in Scotland).

"The Beech delights in Mountains" (an exaggerated description of the gentle chalk hills). "It is an high tree," said John Gerard in his *Herbal* (1597), "with boughes spreading oftentimes in manner of a circle, and with a thicke body having many armes; it groweth very plentifully in many Forrests and desart places" (an equally dramatic description of Sussex and Kent, which he names as its particular haunts). But certainly the beech is a forest creature, and when full grown is too overwhelming for any but a large-scale landscape—a hundred feet high and as much across in open situations, with branches sweeping to the ground in solid masses of foliage. Grown to this noble luxuriance, it is a magnificent tree, clean and healthy in all its parts and in all seasons, from the filmy green of its young foliage to the glowing orange of its autumn leaves. When close-grown as woodland it creates cathedral-like spaces between its smooth iron-grey trunks rising clear from a russet carpet of fallen leaves. (The American beech is very similar, but with striking silver-grey trunk and branches, which are especially beautiful in early spring sunshine.) The beech can be tamed, of course, to suit our domestic landscapes, but it always tends to outgrow and outshade its situation, and in living areas is often best used for one of its incidental qualities—that the young wood holds its dead russet leaves all through the winter, making beech hedges as effective as evergreens for windbreaks. On a larger scale, the same russet winter effect can be produced by periodic coppicing, for the beech sends up new shoots from the base of its trunk when the tree is cut young. The old writers recommend coppicing rotations varying from seven to twenty years, depending on conditions of growth and the height of coppice wanted. Hornbeam (*Carpinus betulus*) also keeps the leaves of young shoots through the winter, but their pale brown is less attractive. The hornbeam, however, is even more tolerant of trimming than the beech, and was the chief tree used for the vegetable architecture of Versailles.

The ash (*Fraxinus excelsior*), like the beech, enjoys a limey soil, but needs a deeper, moister root run to flourish. In drier conditions the foliage is sparser—a desirable quality near buildings—and in any case the ash is a far more adaptable tree. Naturally at home in the open landscape, but equally so in living areas, it is in fact one of the very best trees for urban and suburban landscape, large and impressive, but never of overwhelming mass, since both its branching and its leafing are spacious and open. It also grows naturally with a clear trunk and high head of branches, an important habit in landscapes we live in. The ash is a particularly graceful tree, it creates elaborately structured spaces within its branches, and its pale silver-green pinnate foliage casts a light dappled shade. The leaves move easily in the slightest breeze, and a curious charm is that in almost still air single leaves will plane constantly to and fro as if some hidden animal were swaying one particular twig. The ash has probably the shortest period of leafing of any of our trees; like the oak, it is proverbially late in spring and also early to retire in autumn—another advantage in areas (near houses, for instance) where only summer shade is wanted. In winter the bold pattern of twigs and branches emphasises the clean-cut quality of this attractive tree, whether outlined dark against the light, or with the sun on the pale grey bark and black winter buds. It is of classical character, elegant and decorative, confident and restrained; it composes excellently with buildings, and to satisfy our impatience is a fast and vigorous grower, especially in its early stages. (Unfortunately, the ash happens to be one of the species least tolerant of damage, particularly in its early stages of growth.)

Limes (lindens, in America) are more commonly planted: they are both native and introduced and have also produced hybrids. The common lime (*Tilia vulgaris*) is much infested by aphids, which drizzle a sticky honeydew on anything beneath—an unpopular habit in urban areas. Other limes are generally free of this—the large and large-leaved *Tilia platyphyllos,* the smaller silver lime (*Tilia tomentosa*), and the handsome *Tilia euchlora* with its lustrous leaves. Limes are heart-shaped trees with heart-shaped leaves, fresh green through the summer, and with luck a clean pale yellow in autumn. The common lime is very long-lived and, being very tolerant of pruning, can be trained into screens, arbours, and so on. "Patient of the scissors," the old gardeners called it, and they considered that a cardinal virtue. One of the chief delights of the limes is the scent of the pale yellow-green flowers in July, enveloping waves of subtly delicious sweetness in warm midsummer weather (lime honey is equally delicious).

The elm (*Ulmus procera*) seems chiefly renowned for capriciously shedding its branches, but how often have we actually known it to happen, and how often with ill effects? Far more serious is its liability to the disastrous Dutch elm disease, recently active again both in England (though present since the 1920s) and for some time in America. Of all our trees the lacy winter branch pattern of the elm is perhaps the most beautiful, especially as it thickens with its purplish flowers in early spring. A further virtue of the English elm is its high-headed growth with a canopy of branches on a pillarlike trunk. This is not true of the wych elm (*Ulmus montana*), a broad, rounded tree without this useful piloti structure. An unexpected quality of the elms, which seem essentially country trees, is their surprising tolerance to some forms of pollution, even when extreme. The Cornish elm (*Ulmus stricta*) and its Jersey cousin are of pyramidal growth and useful as narrow street trees, but no elms should be planted at present with elm disease so sadly devastating old English hedgerows and New England greens.

For small-scale and domestic landscapes the silver birch (*Betula verrucosa*) is unsurpassed, and it is surely because it grows so readily that we do not appreciate its many virtues. For it grows easily and fast almost anywhere in the lowlands (in the uplands it is replaced by the white birch, *Betula pubescens*), is more or less indifferent to soil and climate, and needs only plenty of light; it is in fact a pioneer tree on waste ground and on many other types of woodland. Despite its fragile appearance the birch is a forest tree and exceptionally hardy, yet it might nonetheless have been expressly designed for gardens—neat and small-scale in all its parts, even when a full-size tree; never oppressive near buildings, with its slender branches and small light leaves; unaggressive in character; excellent for limited spaces; and unsurpassed in its habit of composing itself gracefully. It is particularly attractive when several are grown together, either as a single tree with multiple stems or as a group of young trees (and it is best moved small) planted close together to fan out in a beautifully balanced composition. No other tree, in fact, so sensitively adapts itself to the space allotted. The silver birch is one of the best year-rounders of all, with pale young leaves and catkins in spring, summer foliage in constant flickering motion, butter-yellow autumn leaf-fall, and lovely in winter, with the shining white bark of its graceful narrow trunk; its habit of growth is like a plumey fountain falling in swinging nets of purple-brown twigs. The Swedish birch (*Betula dalecarlica*) is a variety with deeply cut leaves but otherwise similar.

Humphrey Repton called the alder (*Alnus glutinosa*) the "aquatick oak," and on a smaller, less-spreading scale it has the oak's angled and picturesque branch form. It is an attractive tree in winter, when its decorative structure is enhanced by its dark bark and the small black cones of the previous year. It is good for wet soils, where it grows naturally, but is not limited to water and was once a very common tree in Britain. The Italian alder (*Alnus cordata*) is particularly useful for poor conditions, such as newly made banks and cuttings.

The willows (*Salix* species) and poplars (*Populus* species) have many common qualities, not least their bewildering habit of hybridisation. Fast-growing trees, generally occurring in moist situations, they are extremely useful in open landscape, where their particular beauties are unsurpassed—above all, their summer foliage and winter stem colouring. The narrow silver leaves of willows shining in the wind are like no other effect in our scenery, a glancing play of light which brings alive the dullest landscape. Poplar leaves, too, are in almost constant motion on their vertically flattened stems, making an unstable angle with the horizontal plane of the leaf. While willows sway, poplars flicker with a rainy-sounding rustle all their own. In all but the stillest weather, poplars and willows are in airy movement, and might have been designed by a benign providence to give lightness and delicacy to the heavy clay plains where they naturally grow.

This flickering, rustling summer life of poplars also makes them excellent companions to live with in towns, though they are best planted away from the bases of buildings, where they may drain the subsoil and crack foundations (an effect more often advised against than observed).

The white willow (*Salix alba*) is a large and graceful native tree with many varieties, which may be listed in catalogues as separate species. The silver willow (*Salix alba* var. *argentea*) is even more silvery than the type; the cricket-bat willow (*Salix alba* var. *caerulea*) has yellow winter bark, and the variety Britzensis a crimson bark, while *Salix alba* var. *pendula* is the weeping willow.

The poplars are equally promiscuous and confusing, and it is necessary to identify only those likely to be used for landscape. The black poplars (*Populus nigra*) are the most useful—large and fast-growing trees with tremulous leaves. The black Italian poplar

The shimmering texture of willows seems meant for water.

The foamy masses of the hoary willow (Salix candida).

(*Populus serotina*) is a particularly vigorous hybrid with two helpful varieties—the well-known Lombardy poplar (*P. nigra italica*) and the particularly beautiful golden poplar (*P. nigra aurea*). The white poplars are less tremulous but more silvery in effect because of the white felt beneath their leaves. The leaves of the white poplar (*Populus alba*) are often lobed, and the tree suckers, especially if cut back. (*Populus alba* var. *bolleana* is a narrower variety.)

The grey poplar (*Populus canescens*) is a larger, faster tree with greyish underfelt rather than white, and it also suckers. A strikingly beautiful tree, it is seldom planted.

The Manchester poplar (*Populus nigra* var. *betulifolia*) is a useful tree for polluted city areas, fast and thrivingly healthy in extreme conditions, such as in the many industrial towns of northern England. In the past it was almost the only green which relieved those unlovely brick deserts.

Of our full-size native trees only the larger of the wild cherries, the gean (*Prunus avium*), would popularly be considered a flowering tree. Often as tall as the beeches with which it grows, its blossom is very fleeting. It is one of the few plants improved by doubling, as it is in the garden form.

By purist standards our much-hybridized poplars and willows are doubtfully native, and what of trees like the sycamore (*Acer pseudoplatanus*) and the horse chestnut (*Aesculus hippocastanum*), which are alien introductions, though now generally considered as part of our flora? Gerard describes the sycamore: "The great Maple is a beautifull and high tree, it sendeth forth on every side very many goodly boughes and branches, which make an excellent shadow against the heat of the Sun, upon which are great, broad, and cornered leaves, much like to those of the Vine. The great Maple is a stranger in England, onely it groweth in the walkes and places of pleasure of noble men, where it especially is planted for the shadow sake, and under the name of the Sycamore tree."

That was in the seventeenth century, but since then the sycamore has established itself all over Britain, often replacing the local trees and sometimes becoming a tiresome weed. It is fast-growing, will grow almost anywhere, and is useful as a vigorous tree for poor conditions and as a first line of defence in windbreaks. Its long pink buds are attractive in spring, and so are its hanging green flowers, and with age it develops the tiered branching habit of many of the maples. But its foliage is often coarse and troubled with pests by midsummer, while its excessive fertility can be a

Weeping willows, fastigate poplars, level water (*Kensington Gardens*).

nuisance. It is helpful, however, as a fast-growing tree, especially in its early stages, and when mature has a fine distinctive habit, especially when seen from a distance.

The horse chestnut, an early seventeenth-century introduction, has three good qualities (four if we count conkers for small boys): its candelabra flowers for which it is most admired, its spectacular opening "sticky buds" in spring, and—in the right place—its dense vegetational mass with no sign of any woody structure. No other tree, not even the beech or the sweet chestnut (*Castanea sativa*), gives so solid an effect of absolute mass in the landscape—a strikingly dramatic quality when rightly used, which it seldom is. For the chestnut is not a tree to live with; in detail it is coarse and unattractive, and unless in deep moist soil it is generally in trouble before summer is over. It is not a good town tree either in character or constitution, and in dry seasons its leaves begin to fall in high summer. The sweet chestnut is useful because it is happy on hot dry soils and makes a noble tree, but it needs plenty of room and is not often planted. The loss of the chestnut in the United States is still remembered by some Americans.

The Norway maple (*Acer platanoides*) is another introduction. It is a more elegant tree than the sycamore but also fast-growing and an equally prolific seeder in soils it likes. It is probably best known for its very early vivid yellow flowers on the still-bare twigs, but it is a useful and attractive tree and does well in towns, even in areas of high traffic pollution. William Marshall admired it at the end of the eighteenth century: "The Norway Maple grows to a large tree, Its leaves are of a silvery green colour and are as large or larger than those of the Sycamore; their edges are acutely and more beautifully indented; they are not so liable to be eaten by insects in the summer, and in autumn they die to a golden yellow colour which causes a delightful effect. The flowers are also beautiful; they come out early in the spring, are of a fine yellow colour, and show themselves to advantage before the leaves come out."

The London plane (*Platanus acerifolia*) must surely count as a native, for it appeared in an Oxford garden in the seventeenth century, probably as a spontaneous hybrid between the Occidental and Oriental planes. If Xerxes fell in love with an Oriental plane, he would certainly fall in love with the London version, for in its context it must be one of the most beautiful trees in the world. For cities it is unsurpassed—a huge giant of full forest stature to compose with large buildings, yet of open habit and carrying its branching head of foliage as a leafy roof high above the arched spaces beneath. It is decorative and elegant in all its parts and with no "off-season," which befits a tree we live with as an urban companion all year round. As the spring leaves open like pale green stars the bark peels off the huge smooth trunks in dapple patterns of creams and browns, and in summer the large and shapely leaves sieve the sunlight onto pavements in the same shifting dapples. And though the foliage is luxuriant it does not hide the springing structure of the boughs within. In autumn the large yellow leaves drift down in zigzags one by one; but best of all are planes in winter, their angled twigs and branches elaborately decorative and hung with dangling pompom fruits. They are equally at home with buildings as background or on their own green territory, and in the soft hazy light of London's winters the vistas across the parks are astonishingly beautiful—receding views of tasselled filigree in black and grey, like a Chinese brush painting.

And all this in the direst pollution of nineteenth-century cities, for though with present clean-air controls the sunshine figures for London are now the same as the surrounding country, and few

Planes shaped to form a high canopy and thinned to let in the light (Berkeley Square, London).

London children today have seen a proper fog, London's planes have survived the worst that the past could do. These gloriously healthy giants from the eighteenth century have flourished through Dickens's pea-soupers and the lung-corroding air of last-century London. Looking up into a plane's soaring branches and knowing no better, we might think that dirty industrial cities were the ideal habitat for huge and flourishing forest trees.

Events, they say, produce the man, and cities have certainly produced the tree. The plane seems expressly designed for the benefit of city centres. It is certainly being planted in quantity in New York, where it seems to survive the climate as well as the pollution, and in another generation will transform that largely treeless city. As a town tree it has only two disadvantages—it grows relatively slowly, although in time very large, and it needs room to develop. If planted in confined spaces it is likely to suffer the horrible mutilations we so commonly see around towns.

Of our other natives two small flowering trees are commonly planted: the white-flowered red-berried mountain ash (*Sorbus aucuparia*), a good town tree for small spaces with its attractive pinnate leaves; and the whitebeam (*Sorbus aria*), grown for its white-felted opening leaves like arboreal tulips—a delightful effect on the edge of beech woods on the chalk, where it belongs, but fleeting and unsuited to towns, where it is often planted and seldom thrives. These and other small-scale natives should always be grown on their own roots, for since they grow easily from seed there is no need for grafting them on other species as is often done, a practice which tends to produce a thicket of suckers at ground level from the natural root stock.

An attractive small tree which is seldom planted is our native crab apple (*Malus pumila*). The more flowery garden forms are common, but for open landscape the native species on its own roots is a shapelier longer-lived tree with both flowers and fruits. Another of our smaller trees, the hawthorn (*Crataegus monogyna*), is unrivalled as matrix in the English landscape and is as typical as the oak. It is at home anywhere, the essence of the country in open landscape, but useful also in towns, a neat-growing shrub, bushy to the ground but making a picturesque low-headed tree when old. The garden forms of hawthorn with coloured and double flowers are much less desirable.

The field maple (*Acer campestre*) is a small-leaved small tree of country character which may colour vividly in autumn. The pussy willow (*Salix caprea*) alone of the willows is a tree of dry soils. It is much loved for its early silver, then yellow, catkins (only male trees turn yellow), but undistinguished in summer, with its broad, unwillowlike leaves. Another very early flowering native is the bullace (*Prunus insititia*), which is like a taller, more open, and larger-flowered blackthorn without the spines. It could be used far more than it is for early blossom in wilder landscapes.

It will be noted that some of the trees described above are not indigenous to Britain but have survived in the ecology by virtue of their natural power to reproduce and have been absorbed to the extent of becoming acceptable in the natural landscape.

There are other introduced trees which, though less useful for general planting, are highly successful for urban and green urban situations. Of these, the acacia (*Robinia pseudoacacia*) is particularly useful, for with its sparse open-branching habit it is never oppressive, even near buildings, and casts only a light shade. It has early summer flowers like white laburnum, but far more beautiful is the delicate bright green foliage which stays fresh throughout the summer—"the genteelist tree of all," Horace Walpole called it. It prefers a light soil, not too limey, and though its brittle branches are easily broken in wind the tree seems not to suffer. In open landscape it will produce tall suckering thickets of new growth from the spreading roots, especially if the main trunk is cut down. Its only drawback is that whole boughs suddenly die when the tree is mature.

The tree of heaven (*Ailanthus glandulosa*) is also a good town tree (and also suckers). It is indifferent to pollution, is best in the south, and in late summer the female trees carry bunches of red keys. The Manna ash (*Fraxinus ornus*) is a smaller, bushier tree than our native ash, but with the same elegant leaves. It has yellow-green swags of flowers in June and stands considerable pruning. The Indian bean (*Catalpa biquonioides*) is a low, wide-spreading tree which enjoys the sheltered climate of towns and is a late-summer flowerer. For narrow spaces or vertical accent fastigiate forms of trees may be useful, though their shape is seldom as attractive as the natural branching habit. The beech and hornbeam both have fastigiate forms, and with more space the Lombardy poplar is a good tree, although it suffers from overplanting and its common association with gasometers. It is also susceptible to canker.

The problems of trees in towns are not limited to space. There is still the question of pollution, especially in industrial areas

The light foliage pattern of acacia makes it ideal with buildings and in living areas.

Catalpa in a city centre. (Piccadilly, London).

with harmful fumes. What plants will tolerate the various poisons in problem areas will clearly depend on the climate and the particular pollution, and there is considerable specialised literature on the subject, as there is also on what plants will tolerate the various soil conditions of reclaimed spoil heaps, subsoil, newly made ground, and other unpromising situations. Some plants are more generally immune than others, but nothing is more reliable than seeing for oneself what is actually growing in any given area. Any long-established plants have clearly survived the local pollution and are likely to tolerate all but the worst we offer them.

A list of plants that could be tried in problem areas might include those I saw growing in a small park in a highly industrialised city area surrounded by a gasworks, a power station, a chemical factory, and various other air-poisoning installations. The pollution was so high that despite a mild moist climate grass would not grow, plants came into leaf a month late and lost their leaves a month early, and even the glass of nearby windows turned black and opaque. Nonetheless the park was a leafy green oasis, and some plants were positively thriving. Of trees, the Manchester poplar was doing well, the ash, sycamore, and elm were moderately happy, while the plum-leaved thorn (*Crataegus prunifolia*) was so cheerfully at home that it had not only flowered but set fruit.

Other plants doing well in less extreme conditions in the same city were flowering cherries (sulphur dioxide controls silverleaf), crabs, hawthorns, and sorbus; also London planes and Lombardy poplars, but not birch or beech or horse chestnut, and no one seemed to have tried the oaks.

SHRUBS

Native shrubs should play a large part, for both practical and visual reasons, in our more "natural" designs. It is obviously easier to establish a plant which actually wants to grow than to coax a reluctant stranger to take over alien soil, and in large-scale amenity planting, where linking out to the countryside and preservation of local landscape identity must have high priority, results will be best achieved by planting native species.

In considering the virtues of shrubs it will be useful, while assessing their intrinsic qualities of form, colour, texture, and habit, also to take note of their value within the time scale of the seasons. A landscape can be considered in five main seasons, and if we live with it all the year round each of these should be attractive. The seasons are winter, very early spring, spring with early summer, late summer, and autumn. These are not periods datable on calendars but seasonal effects in the landscape, and in the variable English weather they may be telescoped or protracted or even combined. When a long cold spring, for instance, is followed by warm growing weather, everything will flower together in a great rush of blossom, as if a door had been suddenly opened on a crowd of impatiently waiting guests.

WINTER

Of the five seasons, winter is the most important for design, partly because it lasts the longest but chiefly because unless the design is good the landscape will not be attractive.

Britain is well served with winter vegetation, especially in the beautiful branch patterns of deciduous trees and in the bright evergreen ground cover of grass. We also have two good conifers—the Scotch pine (*Pinus sylvestris*) and the yew (*Taxus baccata*)—and two excellent broad-leaved evergreens, the holly (*Ilex aquifolium*), with its varied habit and foliage, and the ivy (*Hedera helix*), the only hardy evergreen climber. (There is also box—*Buxus semper-virens*—which is rather specialised.)

"The Holly," says William Marshall, "will grow to 30 or 40 feet high with a proportionate stem, which frequently shoots up naked and silvery, six or eight feet high, supporting a close snug elliptical head. This may be called its tree state. But the holly almost as frequently puts on a very different appearance; feathering from the ground and rising with irregular loose, elegant outline, forming one of the most *Ornamental* evergreens which Nature has furnished us with. What renders it peculiarly valuable—it is not only highly ornamental singly or in groups standing in the open, but will flourish with great beauty under the shade and drip of the more lofty deciduous tribes." All this without even mentioning the berries for which most people value holly.

Apart from these paragons, however, England's native flora lack evergreens and winter-flowering shrubs, and we must rely on introduced aliens. Of broad-leaved evergreens the holm oak (*Quercus ilex*) grows slowly in warm districts to a large and massive tree, the Portugal laurel (*Prunus lusitanica*) to a wide near-tree-height shrub with distinguished foliage and habit (it should certainly be planted more often). For hardy, fast-growing, flowering, and fruiting shrubs up to 12 or 15 feet high, the large cotoneasters are invaluable and completely at home with England's vegetation. *Cotoneaster henryana* is the largest-leaved and most upright, *C. lactea* and *C. salicifolia* the best berried, and its varieties (*floccosa* and *rugosa*) more vigorously upright than the type.

For underplanting in woodland, where the shrub layer must form the ground cover, common laurel (*Prunus laurocerasus*) can be both effective and practical. It can either be kept at two or three feet by occasional cutting by machine or, when the trees are large enough, left to grow freely. In damp acid soils, the common rhododendron (*Rhododendron ponticum*) can also form massive ground cover in woodland, though care must be taken, as it can become unmanageable. These large evergreen shrubs have great value in the winter landscape. For colour we can rely on such natives as the hazel with its yellow catkins, the dogwoods with dark purple (*Cornus sanguinea*), bright red (*Cornus alba*), and yellow (*Cornus stolonifera* var. *flaviramea*) stems, and various of the shrubby willows, which also have stem colour. With so much colour available the disposition and balance must be carefully worked out, particularly since many of these shrubs have value only as mass later in the year. Also the need for maintenance should be remembered, as the dogwoods and willows must be cut back thrice yearly to sustain the coloured effect.

EARLY SPRING

In the second season, very early spring, in Britain our native shrubs bullace and pussy willow come into flower as well as various trees which are mostly unnoticed. However, most of our vegetation is not tricked into growth when spring weather comes in February. There is no guarantee that March will not bring winter again, and most of our natives wait cautiously until the end of March or April. At the drab end of winter we long for flowers as at no other season, and there are plenty of introductions which seem perfectly happy in our changeable but mostly mild springs, "for if our Seasons are something more uncertain than they are in other Countries, we have no occasion to repine," said Stephen Switzer, "since the general Temperature of our Climate makes sufficient amends."

In early spring are all the early promises of gardens, especially the vivid pink almond (*Prunus amygdalus*), flowering from bare branches in a bare season, and the myriad-flowered cherry plum (*Prunus cerasifera*), generally planted in its purple-leaved variety (*Prunus pissardii* var. *nigra*), although better with its natural green small-leaved foliage. It is a good, bushy, small tree for "natural" landscape, as is the February-flowering cornelian cherry (*Cornus mas*).

Of shrubs the forsythias are indispensable, even though overplanted and in foreground positions not justified by their dull shapelessness for the rest of the year. *Forsythia ovata* is the earliest, *Forsythia suspensa* the most attractive, the popular hybrids the most flowery and vigorous. The early viburnums, currants, and so on are almost equally vigorous and hardy (the single Jew's mallow, *Kerria japonica,* is a pretty shrub not often enough seen, long-flowering with neat small leaves and thickets of green stems in winter). Of shrubs, in fact, there is no shortage, and of flowers there is a wealth, all the small early bulbs which follow the snowdrops and make carpets of colour from February to March and the drifts of daffodils.

Almost as welcome as early flowers are early green leaves, and everyone loves the pale cascades of the weeping willow when other trees are still bare. Some shrubs too are early leafers, some of the rugosa roses, osoberry (*Nuttallia cerasiformis*), with its greenish-white currantlike flowers, and the useful *Sorbaria sorbifolia*, discussed later and for other qualities. Its leaves appear in February like bunches of green flowers along the twigs and seem indifferent to frost.

LATE SPRING AND EARLY SUMMER

In late spring and early summer there is such an abundance of flowers and new leaves that we can scarcely go wrong. Nearly all our natives and most of our favourite introductions and garden forms are then at their fresh and flowery best, and the difficulty is not in producing landscapes attractive at these seasons, but in finding a place in the year-round design for the ravishing May–June beauties which are so often dull for the rest of the year. For most plants are attractive in flower, as most girls are attractive at parties. But what about the rest of existence? The true beauties are still attractive on disenchanted winter mornings. In flower, philadelphus is irresistible, but dull and ungainly otherwise, and so alas are many of our flowery favourites. And if we can have only a limited wardrobe, it's no good limiting it to a party dress for once-a-year celebrations. Party dresses are to add to wardrobes already well planned, with clothes for all day and every day, and in landscape equally the short-term beauties should decorate a design which is satisfactory without them.

LATE SUMMER

Herbaceous flowers are difficult in design for similar reasons: when out of flower they are often dull, sometimes unsightly, and most of the year invisible. However, for millions of satisfied gardeners very sensibly unconcerned with theories of design, the wealth of flowers from all over the world that flourishes through our gentle summers provides endless colour and interest throughout the late summer period. In the nongarden landscape, late summer can be a dull time of almost uniform heavy green. The native shrubs and trees are busy ripening their seed before the winter, though our native traveller's joy (*Clematis vitalba*) is an exception, and on limey soils it smothers hedges with its waxy cream flowers in August, followed by fluffy white seed heads. Most late-summer flowers are aliens introduced from different climates. Of flowering trees, the Indian bean (*Catalpa biquonioides*), with its broad leaves and horse-chestnut-like flowers, is a low-spreading tree that does well in the south and is useful in towns, although usually planting the late-flowering shrubs is more acceptable.

LATE-FLOWERING SHRUBS

A good, but neglected, group is the eastern privets. *Ligustrum lucidum* is a large shrub or bushy small tree used in southern Europe as a street tree. It has evergreen camellia-like leaves and is covered in August and September with large white panicles of flowers like a species lilac. It is hardy, but best in warm areas, since otherwise frost may overtake its flowers before they open. The Chinese privet (*Ligustrum sinense*) is earlier, and reliably smothered in July with foamy white masses of blossom. It makes a large broad bush and is semi-evergreen.

The dwarf buckeye (*Aesculus parviflora*) is a hardy suckering shrub which makes a wide dome-shaped bush eight feet or more high with candlelike spikes of white flowers in August. Also effective from July on is the smoke bush (*Rhus cotinus*), with its clean rounded leaves and the smother of fluffy seed heads which give it its name.

An English garden in the summer.

Aesculus parviflora *in late summer. A suckering shrub used in high-maintenance design by letting it fill a circumscribed space (Kew).*

Late-summer landscape effects.

The purple-leaved variety is the most popular, the green-leaved pink-headed form the most attractive. "A pretty shrub for Wilderness works," is William Marshall's description of bladder senna (*Colutea arborescens*), with its light pinnate foliage and yellow pea-flowers. It grows anywhere, and if cut back in winter, flowers till the frosts. *Colutea orientalis* is smaller, with glaucous leaves and brown in the flowers.

Of the bold-flowered late shrubs *Buddleia davidii* is the best known and is irrepressible—it colonised London's bomb sites, and it thrives on railway embankments. The purple flower spikes are handsome and deliciously scented, and its somewhat ungainly habit is improved by pruning. (Its popular name of "butterfly bush" depends on butterflies surviving our modern herbicide-pesticide methods.)

The Spanish broom (*Spartium junceum*) is one of the best summer flowers, with its lavish sunburst of clear yellow flower spikes which if sliced off after the first flowering are followed by new growth that flowers till frost. (It also has the added winter bonus of bright green leafless stems.) Like most brooms, it is short-lived but fast-growing, excellent for quick effect. Unlike brooms in general, it thrives on limey soils.

Late shrubs like the veronicas, fuchsias, hypericums, and so on belong to the flower border and are only doubtfully hardy, but there are still the shrub roses, and though most of them flower only once in June some, like the Bourbons and hybrid musks, continue through the summer. The vigorous and self-supporting rugosas are probably the most useful—the single type a very botanical-looking rose, like a drawing of the species for a garden flora. Its pink flowers are followed by large orange hips like small tomatoes. Some of the double crosses also flower all summer, such as roserie de l'haie, which makes a dense large bush about six feet high with continuous clusters of flowers whose unmistakable colour (a deep and vivid violet-red) can be either a triumph or a disaster. For the bold it combines dramatically with the yellow of Spanish broom, and both flower all summer; for the more wary it can be used in large loose groups with the rose-pink Bourbon Zepherine Drouhin (the thornless rose) and her smaller paler sister Kathleen Hartop. Both of these flower on and off through the summer, and the three compose well together in colour and habit, needing no pruning except the old wood cut out.

For landscape where maintenance is minimal, few introduced shrubs are as useful as the sorbarias (formerly known as spiraeas) with their pinnate leaves and large pointed heads of white flowers in July and August. They are excellent foliage plants, good flowering shrubs because of their late season, and though never coarse are of excellently vigorous growth. *Sorbaria arborea* is the best known, a gracefully arching shrub ten feet or more high with huge loose panicles of flowers. It is usually grown as a specimen, but it also spreads by suckers, a habit more marked in two other species—*Sorbaria aitchisonii* and *S. sorbifolia. Aitchisonii* is extremely vigorous; it grows everywhere, making large spreading clumps up to ten feet high with constant new shoots from the base, and soon creates indestructible thickets of its very decorative growth. The elegant pointed leaves are a soft light green, and since the season's shoots continue with fresh growth all summer, the plant is never dull. No other introduced shrub is more generally useful. *Sorbaria sorbifolia* is less vigorous and less tall (three to six feet), but it suckers more widely and makes spreading low thickets with the same light pinnate leaves and smaller panicles of flowers. Both flourish without help, suppressing or tolerating long grass and other plants, and if they grow untidy can simply be cut back at any time during the winter to make vigorous new shoots again the following spring.

Flowers will probably always be popular, but the real effects of the late summer landscape depend on the vegetation as a whole, either on habit and foliage or as material for the design. Contrasts of layers and of massing and spacing are particularly important; so is the use of light and shade and the patterns of shadows. These are the most beautiful effects of late summer, and they depend on the structure of the vegetation and the skill of the designer. On a smaller scale the actual foliage becomes important—the contrasts and groupings of leaves of various shapes and greens—and this is why no description of a plant is useful unless it includes the foliage.

COLOURED FOLIAGE

The natural greens of leaves vary widely from the usual deep green to ash pale, acacia vivid, and so on, as already described. The variations, however, are often too subtle to satisfy our modern taste for strong colour, and mutations with coloured leaves tend to please us more. These are listed in most catalogues, but not all are of equal merit or vigour. Of yellows, the much-scorned golden privet (*Ligustrum ovalifolium* var. *aureo-marginatum*) is actually one of the best, a tall spreading shrub when left to grow naturally instead of to its usual fate of being chopped into hedges, and unlike choicer variegated evergreens a fast and vigorous grower. Nor should the equally scorned spotty laurels (*Aucuba maculata*) be forgotten for difficult conditions in towns and under trees where little else will grow. The gold and white variegated dogwoods (*Cornus alba* vars. *spaetii* and *variegata*) can be useful deciduous shrubs, the box elder (*Acer negundo*) is a bushy small tree with similar variegated varieties, and the variegated Norway maple (*Acer platanoides* var. *drummondii*) is a larger tree, generally healthy and of good habit.

By far the best of all coloured trees is the golden poplar (*Populus nigra* var. *van geertii*), which is not variegated but a soft and variable greenish yellow that blends happily with the greens of the landscape. Unlike many trees with coloured leaves, it is also vigorous and healthy and has all the other attractions of the poplars—the good habit and branch pattern and fluttering leaves. Of shrubs the golden elder (*Sambucus nigra* var. *aurea*) is similarly variable rather than variegated and will grow anywhere. The cut-leaved

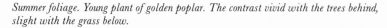

Summer foliage. Young plant of golden poplar. The contrast vivid with the trees behind, slight with the grass below.

golden elder is a different species (*Sambucus racemosa* var. *plumosa aurea*) and does better in the cooler moister conditions of the north, where it is much planted.

Various other trees and shrubs have leaves entirely yellow, for example, the golden acacia (*Robinia frizia*), so popular at present. Usually they are less than enthusiastic growers, since yellow leaves lack most of the chlorophyll on which the plant's life depends. In general yellow-leaved plants do best in sun, white variegations in part-shade. To provide variety in a green landscape, yellow foliage needs careful placing to make its effect. Against grass, it scarcely registers, since grass itself is a vivid and yellowish green and the natural green form of a plant gives a stronger contrast. For yellow foliage to register strongly it needs a dark background—either darker foliage or shadow.

Of colours other than cream or yellow, many consider the liver-reds objectionable, but the copper beech is very popular, and so are the purple plum and the purple smoke bush. Other common trees—sycamore, hazel, Norway maple—have purple varieties.

Silvery and glaucous foliage, on the other hand, is generally the natural colour of plants, and much happier in the landscape than most of the mutations. Willows are among the most beautiful and come in all sizes, from the tall native white and silver willows to the low and spreading hoary willow (*Salix incana*) with its long very narrow leaves which sway on pliant twigs to show their shining white undersides. This is a particularly attractive shrub or small tree ("refined" is a word one would like to use), easy and fast-growing like all the willows, and should be more often planted.

The white poplar, native to Britain, also keeps the white underfelt of its dark-green notched leaves, especially if cut back to make new shoots each year instead of growing to a single tree. The silver maple from eastern North America (*Acer saccharinum*) is a large silvery-leaved tree that does nicely in England, though it seldom colours well with us in autumn.

The sea buckthorn (*Hippophae rhamnoides*) is a silvery native shrub that was once widespread but now grows chiefly on coastal dunes. It suckers but will make a small tree, and the female plant is very attractive in late summer, with its orange-yellow berries in narrow silver leaves. (Males should be planted at the back of groups to be useful and unseen. They can be distinguished from the females even in winter by their fatter buds.) The thorn *Crataegus orientalis* is a small tree with the same attractive colour scheme of orange berries and silver leaves, but deeply cut (and since it is a species and ripens seed readily, why must it always be grafted?).

The Judas tree (*Cercis siliquastrum*) has attractive round glaucous leaves, though it is generally grown for its pink spring flowers; the willow-leaved pear (*Pyrus salicifolia*) is a small, very bushy, silvery tree; *Rosa rubrifolia* has leaves that are not red but pink-flushed glaucous (it is another possible restraining companion for roserie de l'haie). And many trees and shrubs, though not specifically listed as having coloured leaves, vary from the usual greens. Foliage tends to be pale in limey soils.

For dark foliage many of the evergreens are useful, but none compares with the velvety texture of dark conifers, most especially our native yew (*Taxus baccata*). Its matt black-green makes up the ideal background for brighter colours—its commonest use. The necessary clipping slows its growth, but despite popular belief, the yew is a fast grower if left alone. It makes a wide plumey bush and ultimately a tree. William Marshall considered it "genteel"—"If the *Yew* be suffered to form its own head it becomes ornamental to a superior degree; it throws out its lower branches to a great extent; and shooting upwards, takes a striking conical outline; putting on a loose genteel appearance." Of similar colour but looser texture is the foliage of our native pine (*Pinus sylvestris*). It has the usual conical conifer growth when young, but when mature has a clear trunk and russet bark, if the branches are topped as it grows.

AUTUMN

The last of the year's five seasons is autumn, and though in America the fall is often the most beautiful time of the year, in England it is an unreliable season, especially in the north. It may be a long mellow Keats-like extension of summer lasting almost till Christmas, but just as easily autumn rains may early reduce everything to sodden gloom.

We are in any case less enthusiastic about summer's going than its coming, since in spring we treasure every sign of the approaching warm weather, and every bud and shoot is welcomed not only for itself but as herald of the season ahead. Not so autumn. Should we be as fond of the much-loved snowdrop if it flowered at the start of winter instead of the end? We are choosier too about autumn weather, since after an open-air summer we are less impatient to be out-of-doors, whereas the first mild days of spring bring us out to bask ecstatically in the sunshine.

So although nurserymen's catalogues may be full of plants recommended for their autumn colour, autumn is seldom a satisfactory season to plan for. The colours may well be superb, the autumn fruits as lavishly decorative as any flowers, but nonetheless they do not compare in our affections with early spring blossom. Nor is autumn leaf colour reliable in England; it varies with soils and summers, and even in a good year storms can destroy overnight the fragile beauties of the dying season. Autumn effects should mostly be an added bonus to plants we choose for other qualities, and only a few superlative doers should be chosen for autumn alone.

Of plants with coloured leaves the Japanese maples are the most spectacular, with their flaming reds and oranges, but they are small and slow-growing and dislike lime. Azaleas also colour well and need an acid soil, while the sumacs, viburnums, the gean, various barberries, and so on may or may not die off in spectacular reds. Neither the brilliant American maples nor the scarlet oak colours well in Britain. Our own trees vary with the season and are yellows rather than reds—birches, elms, limes, poplars, Norway maples—while beeches die off in orange and russet, especially on chalk.

Coloured fruit is a more reliable autumn effect, especially in the rose family. There are the species roses themselves, of course, but also our ubiquitous hawthorn and its brighter-fruited cousins, the variously coloured crabs, the pyracanthas and all the reliable and lavishly fruiting cotoneasters.

Of other families the berried viburnums are vivid but soon over; the holly lasts all winter (as does the thorn *Crataegus carrierei*); the spindle tree (*Euonymus europaeus*) has unlikely pink and orange fruits as fascinating as any flower, but it is a dull plant the rest of the year, and very poisonous.

Coloured leaves and fruits are banners of departing summer, but the winter evergreens are just coming into their own. They are as new every autumn as deciduous trees every spring. Most evergreens are at their least attractive in spring and early summer, when their pale new leaves make a piebald effect with last year's dark foliage, and dead leaves are shed unseasonably (it is not the time, for instance, to visit Italian gardens with their new-sprouting ilexes). We feel that evergreens, like animals, should moult and recover out of sight, and certainly all summer they thrive unnoticed to emerge in autumn at their flourishing best, as sleek and healthy in their new season's foliage as birds in their new winter plumage.

And as the deciduous vegetation dies back at the end of summer, the different winter design emerges—the patterns of bare branches against the sky, the groupings massed and thickened with dark evergreens, lightened with the background ground cover of grass, and with here and there subtle winter effects of coloured bark or long-lasting berries or winter flowers. For gardeners who plan well this is the most solidly satisfactory season of all—the garden as beautiful as in summer in its different way, and now mercifully static in its winter hibernation. It now needs no effort for months together; the only activity is to walk round and admire, to sit out in sheltered corners in mild winter sun, and with Christmas once over to watch for the early bulbs.

SPECIAL QUALITIES—SURVIVAL VALUE

As well as the five particular seasons, there are particular functions and situations for which some plants are especially suited. Most gardening books and catalogues have lists for different soils, for sun or shade, dry or moist, and so on, but few are much help about plants as material for different design situations. Some of the important individual qualities and seasonal effects have already been discussed; more mundane virtues like fast growth are important for temporary infilling of long-term planting, in the way foresters use temporary conifers to nurse up deciduous trees in difficult conditions. Many fast-growing shrubs have already been mentioned, but an excellent one much used on the continent and not enough here, perhaps because of its deceptively delicate air, is *Spiraea vanhouttei*. It has neat small leaves, a reliable wealth of white flowers in early June, and makes a bushy branching shrub about six feet high that sends up constant new shoots from the base. For landscape design it is by far the best of the spiraeas.

For places where use is rough or vandalism likely, we also need shrubs as nearly indestructible as possible, both for their own sake and to nurse up trees. Fast and vigorous growth to make good the damage is more effective than the prickles usually relied on, especially if combined with a suckering habit. *Sorbaria aitchisonii* is here a natural paragon, sea buckthorn (*Hippophae rhamnoides*) has spines as well as suckering, and blackthorn (*Prunus spinosa*) makes impenetrable thorny thickets, with white flowers in early spring and purple-black autumn sloes. Ordinary bush and floribunda roses also make unexpectedly effective defences, not because of their thorns but because they are so universally cherished that they often escape harm—either through better feelings in the vandals or popular protection of such treasured favourites. Vandalism apart, many young plants are destroyed through carelessness or because they are quite simply not recognized, and people unknowingly trample down young trees and shrubs while they pick their way round a clump of daffodils. Roses and other easily recognized favourites can be used to protect insignificant permanent planting in the vulnerable early stages and will give a great many people a great deal of pleasure in an otherwise dull and skimpy landscape. And as the long-term plants take over they will in turn be appreciated and cherished, for people will fight to save trees which as saplings they trampled down unheeding.

SUCKERING HABIT

The suckering habit of growth—sending up new shoots from the roots at a distance from the parent plant—occurs in plants of all the layers of vegetation, trees as well as shrubs and flowers. It is usually considered a nuisance, but this is chiefly because the suckers we are most familiar with are from grafted plants and we do not want growth from the root stock. Roses are an obvious example. However, we could fairly say that this is our own misuse of a vigorous plant, and the suckering habit can equally be a merit. In design it has various advantages. It means, for instance, that the spotty effect of the original planting quickly disappears as suckers spread into the gaps, that plants fill a given space with the growth best suited to the conditions, and that where unconfined they will produce thickets of spontaneous growth of different ages and in the plant's intrinsic habit, which means they are more naturally adapted to the landscape than our own arbitrary once-only planting.

At a more mundane level, suckers are clearly a cheap way of producing a number of plants from a single original, and in damage-prone areas the plants are more likely to survive. For when a plant with a single stem is broken, it is probably lost. A suckering plant, if well established, will send up new shoots with reassuring persistence.

In formal planting suckering plants can be difficult, and

Sorbaria aitchisonii, *eight feet high. One year's growth from an old clump cut back to near ground level the previous winter.*

The suckering habit in trees. Acacia tree on the left with suckers forming a shrublike thicket along the path. Excellent for natural landscape.

The white poplar in a country lane. Aging parent tree on the right, new sucker growth on the left.

certainly they are dangerous neighbours for less vigorous companions. In high-maintenance areas they are probably best used as a single species filling an allotted area. But in "natural" planting and semiwild landscape the suckering habit is invaluable, and in mixed planting where maintenance is marginal it is a simple way of filling intervening spaces that would otherwise grow weeds. Some plants will no doubt be overwhelmed in the process, but those best suited to the conditions will take over and flourish with minimal care.

Many suckering plants that have been mentioned are by no means aggressive. *Berberis stenophylla* spreads by slender arching shoots; *Kerria japonica* and *Symphoricarpos orbiculatus* are also useful. Other suckering shrubs are excellent for large-scale background planting, like the dogwoods with their thickets of coloured stems in winter, while blackthorn will make an impenetrable thicket.

Besides plants which actually sucker, many vigorous shrubs of spreading indeterminate habit can be used in loose masses for natural-style planting in large-scale landscape. Forsythia and philadelphus are good used like this; so also are the vigorous shrub roses like Nevada, and all the rugosas, and hybrids of choicer plants like the somewhat ungainly *Viburnum burkwoodii*. Grown this way, they lose their garden character and seem naturalized. It is a lavishly effective way of using popular flowering shrubs of not good enough year-round habit for close-up areas.

GROUND COVER

Plants for ground cover are always conspicuously listed in catalogues, generally with the implication that they make weeding unnecessary. This is true only in special circumstances, or where the plant suggested is more vigorous than the grasses and flowers (weeds to gardeners) which are the natural ground cover of open space in England. Very few plants hold their own against grass. In full light only low shrubs are really effective, but in shade ivy may take over large areas, and in high shade and between shrubs and trees ground elder (*Aegopodium podagraria*) is an excellent cover not enough used. Subshrubs, especially if evergreen, will grow to a close cover; for instance, rose of Sharon (*Hypericum calycinum*) or *Gaultheria shallon* on acid soils, and the somewhat taller Oregon grape (*Mahonia aquifolium*). The prostrate spreading cotoneasters and junipers are also effective, but need weeding until established. Taller and therefore more self-sufficient is *Lonicera pileata,* a spreading small-leaved evergreen about three feet high which makes an attractive background of fresh bright green all winter and is deliciously lemon-verbena scented in June. Rampant climbers like the Russian vine (*Polygonum baldschuanicum*) can be used to cover anything, including the ground. The results are fast (its popular name is "mile-a-minute") if somewhat untidy, but there are swags of loose creamy flowers in August. The climbing hydrangea (*Hydrangea petiolaris*) is less rampant, though of better character, with its bright heart-shaped leaves and panicles of white flowers. Some roses are also recommended for ground cover, but weeding is necessary and highly unpleasant.

In large-scale landscape any low shrubs can be used as ground cover if vigorous and of spreading habit. So, clearly, can the suckering shrubs already mentioned, especially since the vigorous growers can be cut back mechanically if they get too high, or straggly and thin at the bottom. This is a way of managing vegetation, possible now with modern large-scale cutting machines, which has not yet been generally used but which could be very useful as well as economical. And it is likely that a great many more shrubs than we suppose would adapt to the treatment, since most shrubs have evolved to withstand the grazing of animals, and cutting back is not fundamentally different.

Another important quality allied to value as ground cover is whether shrubs are bushy to the ground. This prevents the growth of weeds, but more important, it gives the planting a solid base and merges it into the land forms. The mahonias, *Laurestinus viburnum*, rhododendrons, Portugal laurel, and yew are some solidly useful evergreens in roughly ascending size. There are many more.

Particularly useful for the edge of mown areas, especially in high-maintenance landscape, are the horizontally branching evergreens that carry their branches clear of the ground and thus leave space for mowing machines to run beneath them. This means that the shrubs can branch freely and naturally over the lawn, with no harsh edges (and no hideous edging) where grass meets beds. Two useful shrubs with this habit are *Juniperus sabina* var. *pfitzeriana*, and the broad-leaved evergreen *Prunus laurocerasus* var. *zabelliana*. Both are handsome and vigorous (the laurel with narrow shining leaves and upright spikes of white flowers in June, the juniper like a feathery sideways explosion), and both eventually become large. For smaller areas, *Lonicera pileata* can be used in the same way by occasionally cutting out the lower branches.

Juniper "pfitzeriana."

Common laurel and machine maintenance as ground cover.

DESIGNING FOR POPULAR TASTE

In industrial cities in the north of England it often seems that a disproportionate number of plants are chosen for their flowers alone. It is easy to understand—after grey decades of smoke and grime—a longing for the brightly coloured and lavishly flowery. Nor is it only in grey cities that flowers are the first popular choice. In public landscape it is part of the designer's job to please people who are not consciously interested in the design but who nonetheless know what they like and enjoy. And what most people like is flowers—as large and as bright and as many as possible.

Even if landscape designers have very different values, they are designing for popular enjoyment, and if their landscapes please only the designers and not the people who use them then they cannot be considered successful. This is not to say that designers should work to the lowest common denominator of popular taste, but that within their overall design they should find room for popular favourites. In England—a nation of flower lovers—the most popular plant is the rose. (In fact, we think it our own national flower, though so do various other countries.) Let us begin by considering what qualities in the multitude of roses available are desirable for landscape design. First, of course, habit: roses of loose bushy growth, but needing no support; of fair size (four to six feet is useful); needing no spraying and minimum pruning; with healthy and attractive leaves; with flowers not too large and preferably flat on the branch, of unaggressive colour, borne singly or in loose sprays, and dropping their petals when dead (an important quality in all flowers).

Many of the species and so-called shrub roses have these qualities, but most of them flower only once, and they do so in the June heyday when choice is wide and their value therefore less. In any case what is wanted is not the popular roses that sell 50 million a year—the floribundas and hybrid teas—which as landscape material are extremely difficult to use. Their flowers are disproportionately large for the size of the plant, held stiffly upwards on erect stalks, and often of harsh and unaccommodating colours. They are grown in beds kept bare of other plants to encourage larger flowers, and for the same reason pruned down to mutilated stumps. This is particularly destructive both of the year-round landscape scene and of the plant's habit, for it destroys their natural loose way of growth.

Nonetheless it is easy to see why these roses are the chief delight of millions of gardeners. They grow easily and well any-where, in almost any conditions, and under virtually any treatment. They produce large and lavish flowers in a wide range of colours, they bloom through the whole of summer and autumn, have at-tractive leaves, and are much prized as cut flowers for the house. It is certainly an impressive list of virtues, and all this in addition to their scent, which is unsurpassed. No odor wafted from lilies or lilacs or syringa or pinks or lavender or any of our other favourites—no matter how delicious in itself—can compare with the subtle, exquisitely blended, never-palling, sad-sweet smell of roses. It is incomprehensible that any scentless rose should ever be a favourite.

Roses are flowers to cut, or at least to see in close-up, and are essentially plants for the garden or small-scale landscape, though even here the pruned-back polyanthuses and hybrid teas are difficult in the design. In the past roses were often grown, with other flowers for picking, in the vegetable garden, where they flourished in the rich soil. In an ornamental garden one way to limit their disadvantages is to grow them with other shrubs and to give them no pruning except to cut out old wood. Grown like this, their flowers are smaller and better proportioned to the size of the bush, and they develop their own habit of growth. Different varieties respond with varying success to this treatment. Iceberg makes a loose bush, pink Queen Elizabeth keeps its strongly upright growth, red Frensham is shrubby, New Dawn makes a bushy mound with endearingly cottagey flowers, and so on. If we have particular favourites it is certainly worth trying them out in this way among other shrubs, but it is still not what is commonly meant by growing roses. Most gardeners do feel that a rose is a rose is a rose, and will always prefer them grown to perfection in rose beds—and bother the landscape design! This is excellent for private gardens, where our own taste is absolute. In public landscape, too, designers must sometimes accept that their job is to provide a good general setting for growing the flowers people want.

Flowering trees such as cherries can be equally difficult to use, though their early and lavish spring blossom makes them irreplaceable—certainly in general affection. Out of flower, how-ever, they are mostly dull or even ugly, for like nearly all our garden forms they are grafted plants, with the various disadvantages in-herent in the process.

GRAFTED PLANTS

Grafting is an unnatural joining of the branch system of one plant to another. It is no wonder that the combination often makes an unsatisfactory whole—like joining the front of a horse to the back of a cow. For a tree is a unity, a coherently organised living entity with its own distinctive character in every part—roots and trunk and branches and leaves and flowers. But a grafted tree is two different growth patterns joined together, and the resulting malformations are various. Instead, for instance, of the branches flowing out from the trunk like limbs from a body, they often shoot out from the graft at ungainly angles (as, for example, the unfortunately popular cherry whose double bright pink flowers are so completely disastrous with its copper-red young foliage—like an umbrella blown inside out).

Often, too, since the root stock is commonly more vigorous than the scion, a solid trunk supports only an incongruously small head of branches, with a congested swelling where the rising sap is checked at the graft. Grafted trees are also commonly short-lived (who can wonder?) and are generally weakened by their determined efforts to make normal growth by putting out branches and suckers of the species their roots are meant for, and which, if left alone, will starve off the alien graft. For a graft is a kind of cancer that a healthy tree will suppress if it can.

Therefore, where cherries, or other trees and shrubs, can be grown on their own roots this should always be done. They make better plants, live longer, and need less care. With some species this is possible by growing plants from seed, with garden forms by layering or cutting. However, it is a slower process than grafting, may not be suitable for trees, and in any case most available plants are grafted.

Grafting is practised for various reasons and justifiable by various standards. One is to produce salable-size plants as quickly as possible (the nurseryman's justification); another, that they grow faster when planted (the impatient gardener's reason); but a more fundamental reason is that many very desirable forms of plants are chance mutations or hybrids difficult, and sometimes impossible, to grow in any other way. Or because a species is not hardy when grown on its own root stock.

One of the common mutations of propagating by grafting is doubleness in flowers. This is a malformation of the reproductive

The horrible deformity of a grafted cherry.

parts to produce petals or partly formed petals. The flowers are completely doubled and are therefore sterile and produce no seed, and so do not survive in nature. Doubling also destroys the natural shape and character of the flower, and although some flowers (roses, for instance) develop a distinctive new growth pattern, many double flowers (daffodils, snowdrops, delphiniums—the list is long) look the distortions they actually are.

Because they are sterile, however, double flowers usually last much longer than single, waiting hopefully for pollination instead of shedding their come-hither petals and settling down to fruitfulness. When it is not individual flowers we are concerned with but the general effect of a blossoming tree, then doubling is a great advantage, since it doubles (or more) the length of flowering. This is so with cherries, and well-shaped double forms are far better garden trees than the briefly flowering single species. They also have the extra advantage that being sterile with no fruit to ripen they can put all their energy into lavish and reliable flowering—built-in dead-heading, in fact.

As for the poor structure of many grafted trees, this can be disguised in various ways. One way with cherries is to use the bush or the half-standard forms and plant them in mixed groups with other trees and shrubs, where their spring blossom shows to advantage against the dark background and the graft is hidden. But much of the pleasure of cherries is their lavishness, the glorious unstinted profusion of their flowering—that whole trees are a mass of bloom, and we can walk beneath the enveloping flowery branches and look up at the sky through the blossoms. So if we want trees, they can be planted among other taller trees of longer-lasting virtue, so that in summer their dullness is lost in the general green background, and in winter their ungainly structure is not silhouetted on the skyline. This is equally true of all trees and shrubs grown only for their flowers, meaning most of the popular favourites. Whatever their siren charms when in blossom they should rarely be planted as specimens, or as street trees, or for any kind of IN planting—certainly the three most common uses of cherries.

IN CONCLUSION

"The art of landscape gardening is the only art which everyone professes to understand, and even to practice, without having studied its rudiments. No man supposes he can paint a

Root suckers from a grafted tree.

Half-standard cherries massed among shrubs.

Cherries among pines for contrast.

Cherries in the open but not on the skyline.

landscape, or play on an instrument, without some knowledge of painting and music; but everyone thinks himself competent to lay out grounds, or to criticise on what others propose, without having bestowed a thought on the first principles of landscape gardening." (Humphrey Repton.)

In our new urban environments we have to go further than this simple (though still valid) plea. Science must play a part too. Already mentioned is the need for research into container planting. Further enquiries are needed on the question of the use of vegetation to lessen wind turbulence in large urban building complexes. We need to know the effect of the turbulence on the plants themselves and the best species to plant. There are other problems which would repay the attention of plant breeders (if they could be persuaded from their seemingly exclusive preoccupation with making flowers bigger and brighter and in colours not natural to them). We need plants that are immune to pollution, to frost, to dry conditions. And in an age when we are even more impatient than Horace Walpole, think what a boon it would be to have trees and shrubs which grew swiftly to mature size and then remained fairly static.

Given any hope of the plant breeders' cooperation, the list could be extended indefinitely. Nor is it entirely fanciful. Many plants have potential genetic variety that is at present unused in the conditions to which they have adapted but which might be developed to suit them to the different conditions we now impose in our changed environment. Modern geneticists are becoming inhumanly clever and already forecast genetic tailoring almost to order; why not use their skills to produce useful plants for the landscape designer?

Index

A Note on the Type

This book was set in film in Baskerville. Baskerville is a
facsimile cutting from type cast from the original matrices
of a face designed by John Baskerville. The original face
was the forerunner of the "modern" group of type faces.

John Baskerville (1706–75) of Birmingham,
England, a writing master with a special renown for cutting
inscriptions in stone, began experimenting in about 1750
with punch-cutting and making typographical material. It
was not until 1757 that he published his first work, a Virgil
in royal quarto, with great-primer letters. This was followed
by his famous editions of Milton, the Bible, the Book of
Common Prayer, and several Latin classical authors. His
types, at first criticized as unnecessarily slender, delicate,
and feminine, in time were recognized as both distinct and
elegant, and his types as well as his printing were greatly
admired. Four years after his death Baskerville's widow sold
all his punches and matrices to the Société Philosophique,
Littéraire et Typographique, which used some of the types
for the sumptuous Kehl edition of Voltaire's works in
seventy volumes.

Composed by York Graphic Services, Inc., York, Pennsylvania.
Printed and bound by Halliday Lithographers, West Hanover,
Massachusetts.

Typography and binding design by Susan Mitchell.

Nan Fairbrother was born in Coventry, England; she attended the University of London and graduated with honors in English. Before the war she married William McKenzie, a London doctor. An adventure in country living with her two young sons on a farm in Buckinghamshire while her husband was serving in the RAF was the subject of her first book, *An English Year.** It was followed in 1956 by *Men and Gardens,* in 1960 by *The Cheerful Day,* an account of London living, in 1965 by *The House in the Country,*† and in 1970 by *New Lives, New Landscapes,* which won the W. H. Smith Annual Literary Award in Great Britain. Though she did not practice, Miss Fairbrother was a member of the Institute of Landscape Architects. She lectured and wrote articles and book reviews on landscape and land use and throughout the last two years of her life worked on this book, which was largely completed at the time of her death in 1971.

Called in Britain *Children in the House** and *The House.*†